Insects &
Spiders

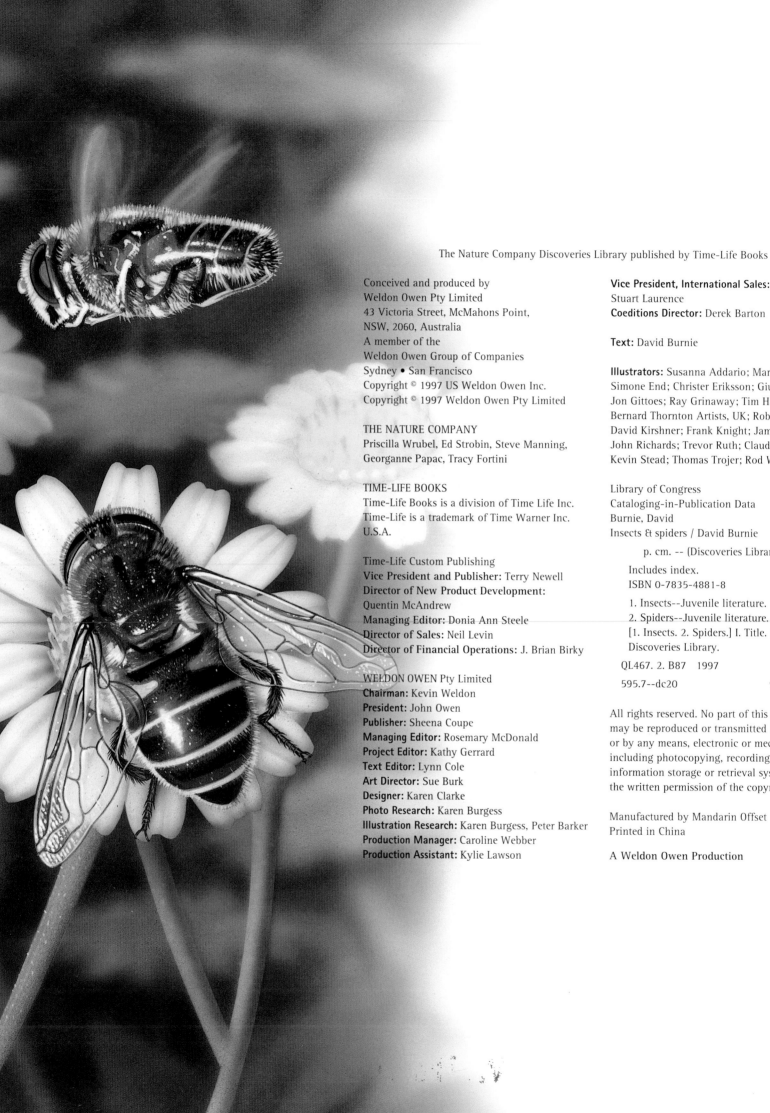

The Nature Company Discoveries Library published by Time-Life Books

Conceived and produced by
Weldon Owen Pty Limited
43 Victoria Street, McMahons Point,
NSW, 2060, Australia
A member of the
Weldon Owen Group of Companies
Sydney • San Francisco
Copyright © 1997 US Weldon Owen Inc.
Copyright © 1997 Weldon Owen Pty Limited

THE NATURE COMPANY
Priscilla Wrubel, Ed Strobin, Steve Manning,
Georganne Papac, Tracy Fortini

TIME-LIFE BOOKS
Time-Life Books is a division of Time Life Inc.
Time-Life is a trademark of Time Warner Inc.
U.S.A.

Time-Life Custom Publishing
Vice President and Publisher: Terry Newell
Director of New Product Development:
Quentin McAndrew
Managing Editor: Donia Ann Steele
Director of Sales: Neil Levin
Director of Financial Operations: J. Brian Birky

WELDON OWEN Pty Limited
Chairman: Kevin Weldon
President: John Owen
Publisher: Sheena Coupe
Managing Editor: Rosemary McDonald
Project Editor: Kathy Gerrard
Text Editor: Lynn Cole
Art Director: Sue Burk
Designer: Karen Clarke
Photo Research: Karen Burgess
Illustration Research: Karen Burgess, Peter Barker
Production Manager: Caroline Webber
Production Assistant: Kylie Lawson

Vice President, International Sales:
Stuart Laurence
Coeditions Director: Derek Barton

Text: David Burnie

Illustrators: Susanna Addario; Martin Camm;
Simone End; Christer Eriksson; Giuliano Fornari;
Jon Gittoes; Ray Grinaway; Tim Hayward/
Bernard Thornton Artists, UK; Robert Hynes;
David Kirshner; Frank Knight; James McKinnon;
John Richards; Trevor Ruth; Claudia Saraceni;
Kevin Stead; Thomas Trojer; Rod Westblade

Library of Congress
Cataloging-in-Publication Data
Burnie, David
Insects & spiders / David Burnie
        p. cm. -- (Discoveries Library)
    Includes index.
    ISBN 0-7835-4881-8
    1. Insects--Juvenile literature.
    2. Spiders--Juvenile literature.
    [1. Insects. 2. Spiders.] I. Title. II. Series:
Discoveries Library.
    QL467. 2. B87   1997
    595.7--dc20   96-28417

Manufactured by Mandarin Offset
Printed in China

A Weldon Owen Production

THE NATURE COMPANY
DISCOVERIES
L I B R A R Y

Insects & Spiders

CONSULTING EDITORS

George Else
& specialist staff
Department of Entomology
The Natural History Museum
London

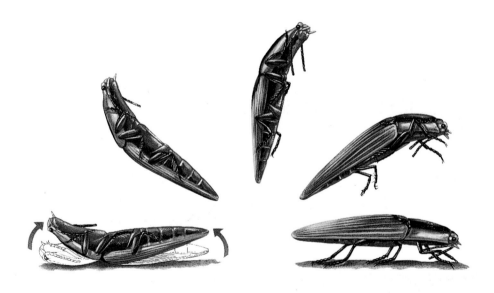

TIME
LIFE
BOOKS

WITHDRAWN
FRIDAY MEMORIAL LIBRARY
New Richmond, WI 54017

Contents

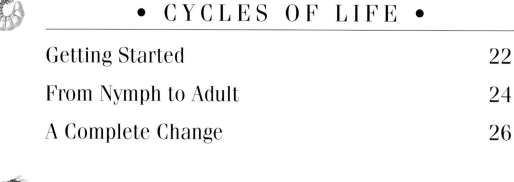

• THE BIG ORDERS •

• INSECTS AND PEOPLE •

• SPOTLIGHT ON SPIDERS •

The Great Success Story

I nsects are among the most successful creatures in the living world. They first appeared more than 400 million years ago, and fossilized specimens, such as the dragonfly at left, show that some have changed little over this time. More than a million species of insect have been identified, which means that they outnumber all other animal species put together. Even more await discovery, and some scientists think that the total number of species may be as high as 10 million. There are several reasons for these tremendous numbers, but the most important is size. Because insects are so small, individuals need only tiny amounts of food. They eat many different things, including wood, leaves, blood and other insects, and they live in a great range of habitats. The survival of insects is also helped by the ability of some to fly, and by their ability to endure tough conditions. Some desert insects can cope with temperatures above 104°F (40°C), and many insect eggs can survive temperatures much colder than a freezer.

TAKING OFF
Insects were the first animals that were able to fly. Cockchafers use their wings to escape danger. This male may also fly far in search of a mate.

UNDERWATER INSECTS
Although insects are common in fresh water, hardly any are found in the sea. This diving beetle is one of many insects that live in fresh water.

LIVING TOGETHER
Many insects gather in groups for part of their lives. This swarm of hungry locusts may have more than a billion individuals, who can munch through huge quantities of food.

THE INSECT ARMY
Scientists divide insects into about 30 different groups, called orders. Insects from some of the most important orders are shown here.

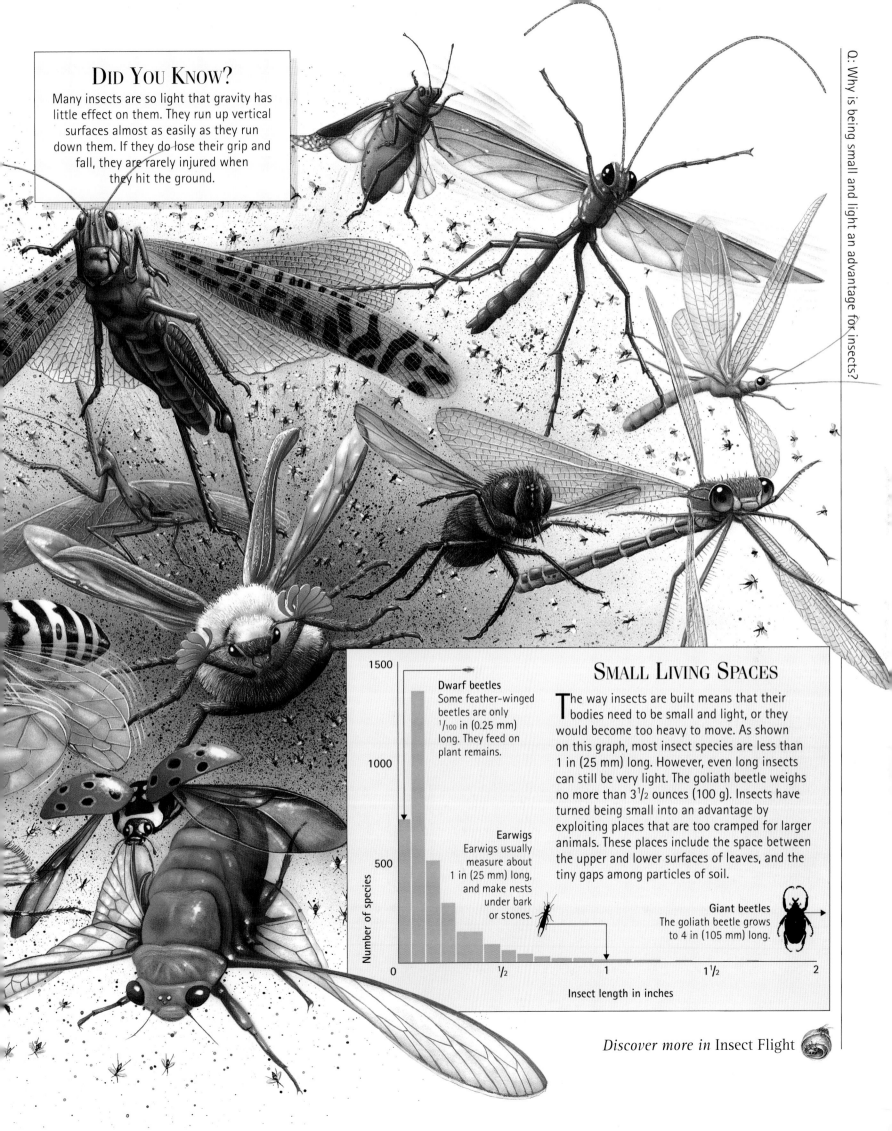

DID YOU KNOW?

Many insects are so light that gravity has little effect on them. They run up vertical surfaces almost as easily as they run down them. If they do lose their grip and fall, they are rarely injured when they hit the ground.

SMALL LIVING SPACES

The way insects are built means that their bodies need to be small and light, or they would become too heavy to move. As shown on this graph, most insect species are less than 1 in (25 mm) long. However, even long insects can still be very light. The goliath beetle weighs no more than 3¹/₂ ounces (100 g). Insects have turned being small into an advantage by exploiting places that are too cramped for larger animals. These places include the space between the upper and lower surfaces of leaves, and the tiny gaps among particles of soil.

Dwarf beetles
Some feather-winged beetles are only ¹/₁₀₀ in (0.25 mm) long. They feed on plant remains.

Earwigs
Earwigs usually measure about 1 in (25 mm) long, and make nests under bark or stones.

Giant beetles
The goliath beetle grows to 4 in (105 mm) long.

Number of species

1500

1000

500

0   ¹/₂   1   1¹/₂   2

Insect length in inches

Discover more in Insect Flight

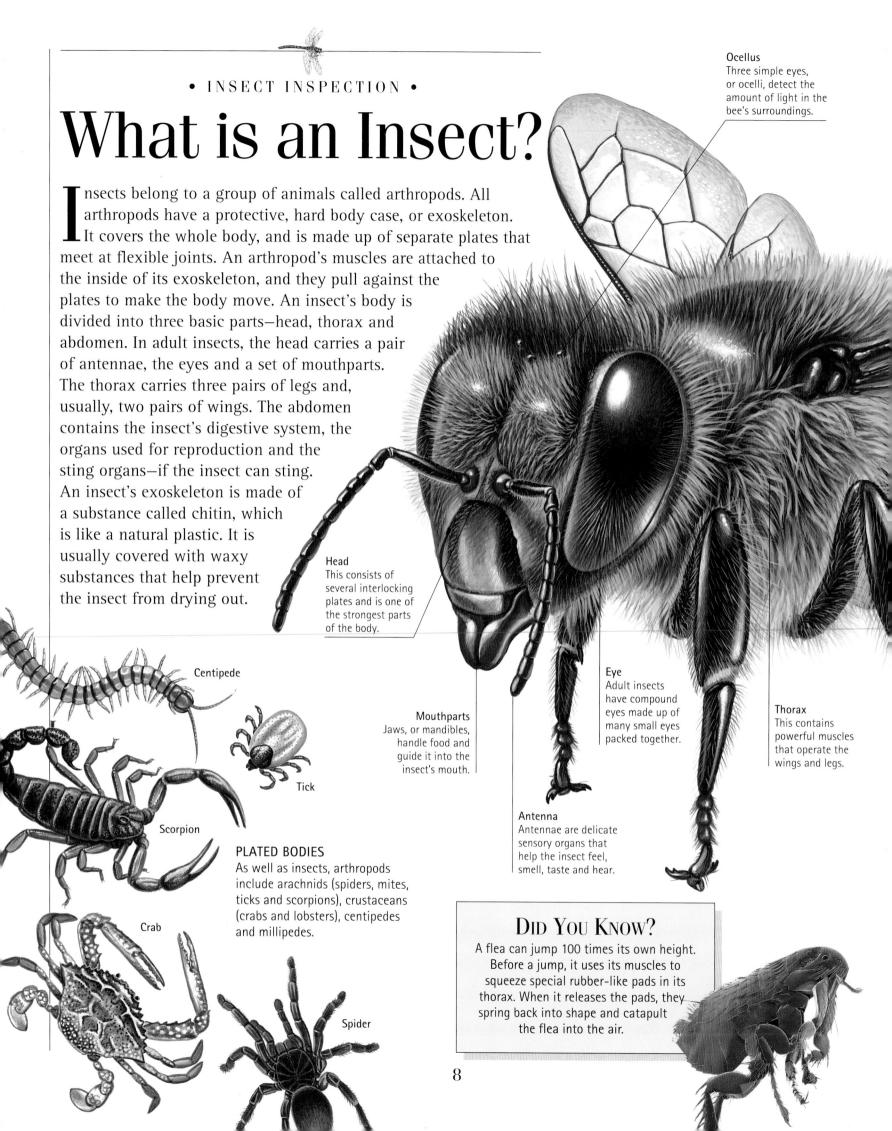

What is an Insect?

Insects belong to a group of animals called arthropods. All arthropods have a protective, hard body case, or exoskeleton. It covers the whole body, and is made up of separate plates that meet at flexible joints. An arthropod's muscles are attached to the inside of its exoskeleton, and they pull against the plates to make the body move. An insect's body is divided into three basic parts—head, thorax and abdomen. In adult insects, the head carries a pair of antennae, the eyes and a set of mouthparts. The thorax carries three pairs of legs and, usually, two pairs of wings. The abdomen contains the insect's digestive system, the organs used for reproduction and the sting organs—if the insect can sting. An insect's exoskeleton is made of a substance called chitin, which is like a natural plastic. It is usually covered with waxy substances that help prevent the insect from drying out.

Ocellus
Three simple eyes, or ocelli, detect the amount of light in the bee's surroundings.

Head
This consists of several interlocking plates and is one of the strongest parts of the body.

Centipede

Tick

Mouthparts
Jaws, or mandibles, handle food and guide it into the insect's mouth.

Eye
Adult insects have compound eyes made up of many small eyes packed together.

Thorax
This contains powerful muscles that operate the wings and legs.

Scorpion

Antenna
Antennae are delicate sensory organs that help the insect feel, smell, taste and hear.

PLATED BODIES
As well as insects, arthropods include arachnids (spiders, mites, ticks and scorpions), crustaceans (crabs and lobsters), centipedes and millipedes.

Crab

Spider

DID YOU KNOW?
A flea can jump 100 times its own height. Before a jump, it uses its muscles to squeeze special rubber-like pads in its thorax. When it releases the pads, they spring back into shape and catapult the flea into the air.

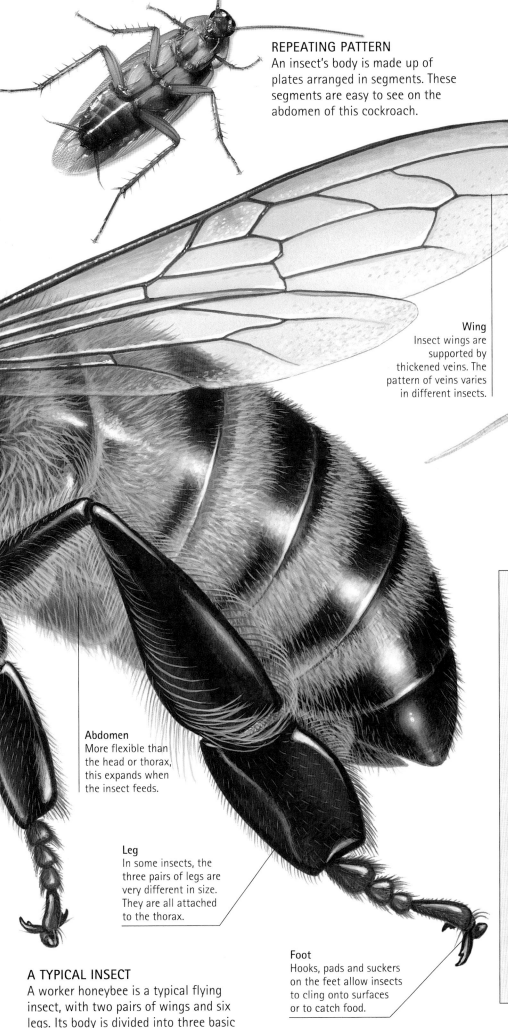

REPEATING PATTERN
An insect's body is made up of plates arranged in segments. These segments are easy to see on the abdomen of this cockroach.

Wing
Insect wings are supported by thickened veins. The pattern of veins varies in different insects.

PRIMITIVE INSECT
A silverfish does not have wings or ocelli. Its flattened body allows it to wriggle into small crevices, even between the pages of a book.

Abdomen
More flexible than the head or thorax, this expands when the insect feeds.

Leg
In some insects, the three pairs of legs are very different in size. They are all attached to the thorax.

Foot
Hooks, pads and suckers on the feet allow insects to cling onto surfaces or to catch food.

A TYPICAL INSECT
A worker honeybee is a typical flying insect, with two pairs of wings and six legs. Its body is divided into three basic parts: the head, thorax and abdomen.

NEW SKINS

Our skeleton grows in step with the rest of our body, but once an insect's exoskeleton has hardened, it cannot become any larger. In order to grow, the insect has to molt, or shed, its "skin," and replace it with a new one. During molting, the old exoskeleton splits open and the insect crawls out. The insect then takes in air or water, so that its body expands before the new exoskeleton becomes hard. Some insects molt more than 25 times, while others molt just twice. Once an insect becomes an adult, it usually stops molting and does not grow any more.

Discover more in Getting Started

9

A Closer View

Inside an insect's body, many different systems are at work. Each one plays a part in keeping the animal alive and in allowing it to breed. One of the largest, the digestive system, provides the insect with fuel from its food. It is based around the gut, or alimentary canal, which runs the whole length of the body. When an insect eats, food is stored in a bulging part of the canal, called the crop. It then travels into the midgut, where it is broken down and absorbed. Leftover waste moves on to the anus and is expelled. The insect's circulatory system uses blood to carry digested food, but not oxygen, around the body. The blood is pumped forwards by a heart arranged along a muscular tube, but it flows back again through the body spaces among the body organs. The nervous system and the brain ensure that all the other systems work together. They collect signals from the sense organs, and carry messages from one part of the body to another.

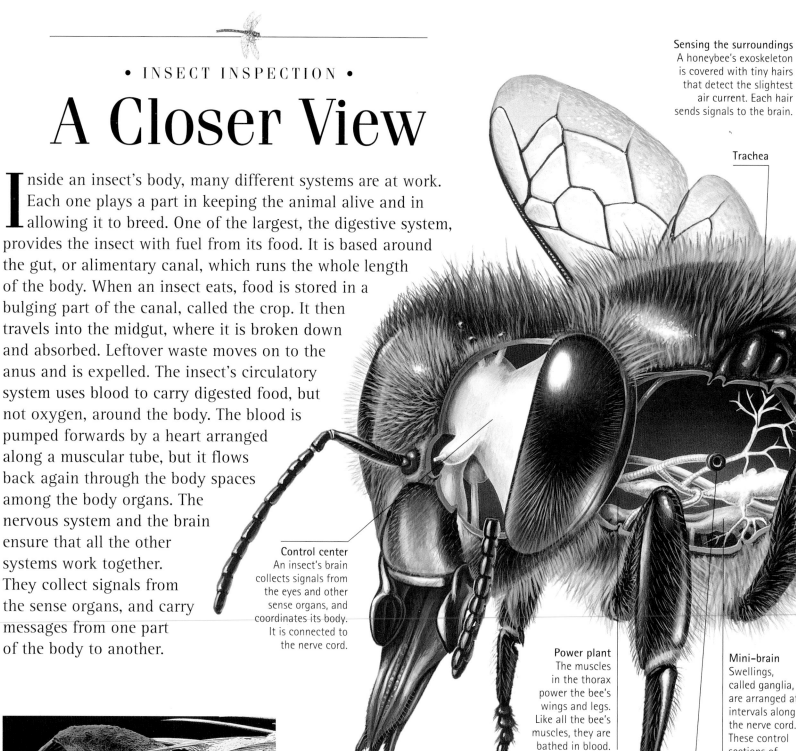

Sensing the surroundings
A honeybee's exoskeleton is covered with tiny hairs that detect the slightest air current. Each hair sends signals to the brain.

Trachea

Control center
An insect's brain collects signals from the eyes and other sense organs, and coordinates its body. It is connected to the nerve cord.

Power plant
The muscles in the thorax power the bee's wings and legs. Like all the bee's muscles, they are bathed in blood.

Mini-brain
Swellings, called ganglia, are arranged at intervals along the nerve cord. These control sections of the body.

Liquid meals
The bee uses its tongue like a drinking straw to suck up sugary nectar from flowers.

INSIDE A BEE
This illustration shows major body systems of the worker honeybee. The digestive system is colored cream, the respiratory system white, the nervous system gray and the circulatory system green.

Air intakes
Openings, called spiracles, let air into the bee's internal air tubes (tracheae). Each spiracle has hairs to keep out dust and water.

GETTING A GRIP
Each fly's foot has a pair of claws and bristly pads. The claws allow the fly to grip rough surfaces, while the bristly pads help it to cling onto smooth surfaces.

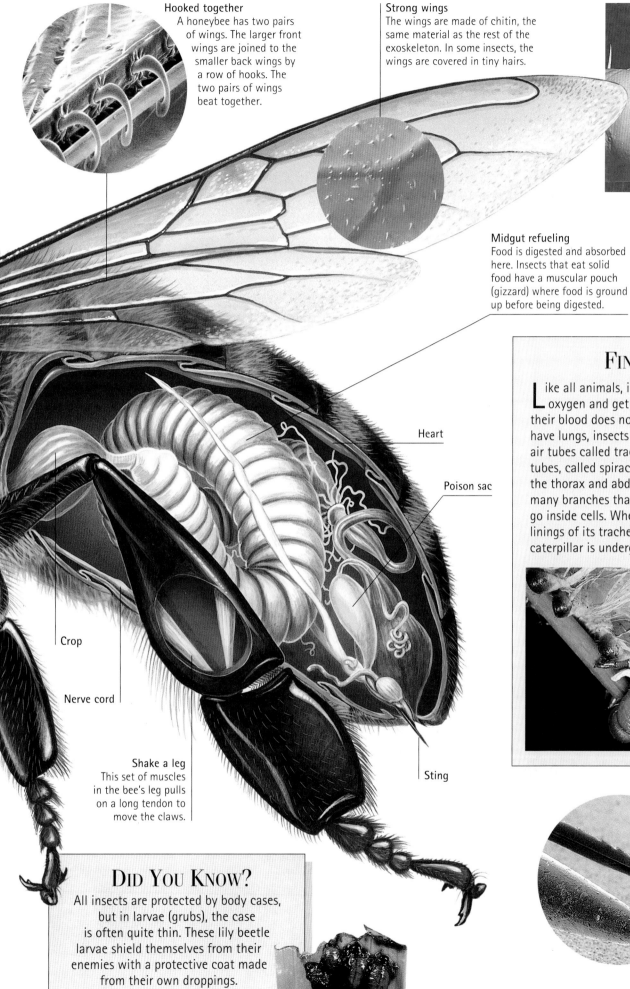

Hooked together
A honeybee has two pairs of wings. The larger front wings are joined to the smaller back wings by a row of hooks. The two pairs of wings beat together.

Strong wings
The wings are made of chitin, the same material as the rest of the exoskeleton. In some insects, the wings are covered in tiny hairs.

FLEXIBLE LEGS
Like all arthropods, an insect's leg has flexible joints that allow the leg to bend. This is the leg joint of a human head louse.

Midgut refueling
Food is digested and absorbed here. Insects that eat solid food have a muscular pouch (gizzard) where food is ground up before being digested.

Heart

Poison sac

Crop

Nerve cord

Shake a leg
This set of muscles in the bee's leg pulls on a long tendon to move the claws.

Sting

FINE TRACHEAE

Like all animals, insects need to breathe—take in oxygen and get rid of carbon dioxide. Because their blood does not carry oxygen, and they do not have lungs, insects breathe with the help of tiny air tubes called tracheae. The openings of these tubes, called spiracles, are located on the sides of the thorax and abdomen. Each trachea divides into many branches that eventually become so fine they go inside cells. When an insect molts, it sheds the linings of its tracheae through its spiracles. This caterpillar is undergoing this remarkable process.

DID YOU KNOW?
All insects are protected by body cases, but in larvae (grubs), the case is often quite thin. These lily beetle larvae shield themselves from their enemies with a protective coat made from their own droppings.

DEADLY WEAPON
A honeybee's sting is like a sharp rod with hooks on it. Once embedded in the skin, the sting releases its poison. Here, the sting (top) is compared to a needle.

Discover more in Insect Senses

The shape of antennae varies among insects, and sometimes even between males and females of the same species.

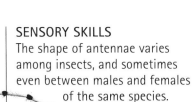

Night-time feeder
A long-horned beetle's long antennae are used for feeling its way in the dark.

Seeking a mate
In flight, a male cockchafer's antennae open out to detect the scent of a female.

Damp skin spots
The human louse uses its antennae to sense damp parts of a body where it feeds on blood.

Air detector
Each butterfly antenna is a slender shaft ending with a small knob. The shafts are covered with hairs that detect air currents.

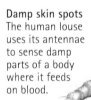

Hot spots
A female mosquito's feathery antennae sense heat from warm-blooded animals. This enables her to find food in the dark.

Feathery sniffer
A male emperor moth can smell a female more than 2 miles (3 km) away.

• STAYING ALIVE •

Insect Senses

To survive, an insect has to know about the world around it. It must be able to find food, track down a mate and, most important of all, detect its enemies before they have a chance to attack. Like many other animals, insects have five main senses—sight, hearing, smell, touch and taste. Each type of insect specializes in using some of these senses more than others. Because dragonflies and horseflies fly during the day, they have large eyes that help them find their victims. Most moths, on the other hand, fly at night. Instead of using sight, they find their food and partners by smell. As well as using senses to find out about the world, insects also have senses that monitor their own bodies. These tell them which way up they are flying, how their wings and legs are positioned, and whether they are speeding up or slowing down. For flying insects, these senses are particularly important.

Human's view

Bee's view

SEEING THE INVISIBLE
Many insects see wavelengths of light that are invisible to us. Above right is how a bee may view a flower. It gives more detail than a human view and guides the bee to the nectar.

12

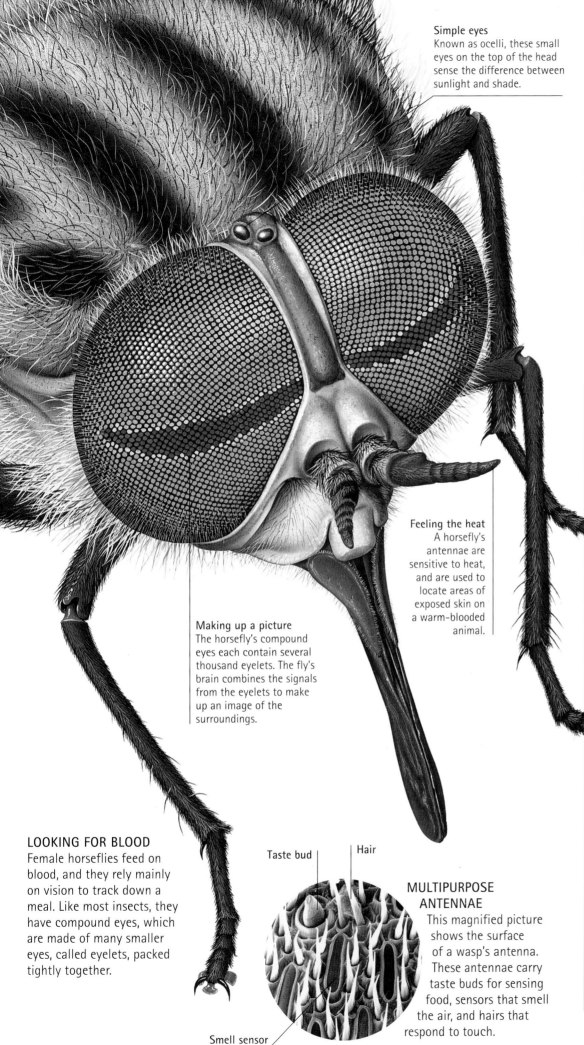

Simple eyes
Known as ocelli, these small eyes on the top of the head sense the difference between sunlight and shade.

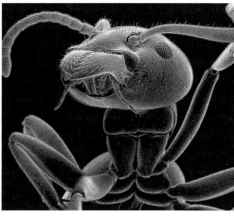

SMALL EYES
The more eyelets an insect has, the more clearly it sees. This wingless worker ant lives in the dark and has small compound eyes, which contain only a few hundred eyelets.

Feeling the heat
A horsefly's antennae are sensitive to heat, and are used to locate areas of exposed skin on a warm-blooded animal.

Making up a picture
The horsefly's compound eyes each contain several thousand eyelets. The fly's brain combines the signals from the eyelets to make up an image of the surroundings.

EARS ON THE BODY
Insects often use their antennae to hear, but they also have other ways of detecting different sounds and vibrations.

Ears on legs
Bush crickets have ears on their front legs. Each ear is a thin oval membrane that moves when the air vibrates.

Feeling the ground
Ants sense vibrations through their legs. They often respond to these vibrations by preparing to attack an enemy.

Ears on the abdomen
Grasshoppers and locusts have ears on their abdomen. They are particularly sensitive to the calls made by their own species.

Leg bristles
A cockroach uses special bristles to sense the vibrations made by something moving towards it.

Wings as ears
The thin and delicate wings of a lacewing pick up vibrations in the air and sense movements.

LOOKING FOR BLOOD
Female horseflies feed on blood, and they rely mainly on vision to track down a meal. Like most insects, they have compound eyes, which are made of many smaller eyes, called eyelets, packed tightly together.

Taste bud   Hair

MULTIPURPOSE ANTENNAE
This magnified picture shows the surface of a wasp's antenna. These antennae carry taste buds for sensing food, sensors that smell the air, and hairs that respond to touch.

Smell sensor

Discover more in Insect Flight

LIVING DRILL
The hazelnut weevil has a long, slender "snout" with tiny jaws at the tip. Using its jaws like a drill, the weevil chews holes in hazelnuts.

Food and Feeding

Individually, insects are quite choosy about what they eat, but together they devour a vast range of different foods. Many insects feed on plants or on small animals, but some survive on more unusual food, including rotting wood, blood, horns or even wool. To tackle each of these foods, insects have a complicated set of specially shaped mouthparts. A praying mantis, for example, has sharp jaws, or mandibles, that stab and cut up its captives, while its other mouthparts help to hold the food and pass it towards the mouth. A grasshopper has similar mouthparts, but its main jaws are much stronger and blunter, and so are ideal for crushing the plant material it prefers. The mouthparts of insects that feed on liquids often look very different than those of insects that live on solid foods. A mosquito has a long stylet that works like a syringe, while a butterfly or moth has a long tongue, or proboscis, which acts like a drinking straw. As this butterfly (above left) demonstrates, the tongue conveniently coils up when not in use.

MIDAIR REFUELING
With its tongue uncoiled, a hawk moth drinks nectar from deep inside a flower. Some hawk moths have tongues that are more than 6 in (15 cm) long.

CHANGING TASTES
Larvae and adult insects often eat very different foods. An adult potter wasp feeds on nectar whereas its larva (left top) feeds on caterpillars.

INSECT MOUTHPARTS

Insect mouthparts are like tools in a toolkit. They are specially shaped to gather particular food and allow it to be swallowed.

Spongy pads
Houseflies use a spongy pad to pour saliva over their food. After the food has dissolved, it is sucked up.

Piercing mouthparts
Female mosquitoes use their needle-like mouthparts to stab through the skin and suck up blood. Males sip only plant juices.

Powerful jaws
Many ants have strong jaws for gripping and cutting up small animals. Some can slice through human skin.

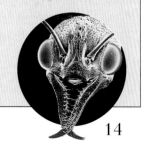

FAST FOOD
A locust chops through a tasty leaf quickly. Its mouthparts, called palps, explore the leaf as it eats.

DID YOU KNOW?

This darkling beetle lives in Africa's Namib Desert, where the only moisture comes from mist rolling in from the sea. To get water, the beetle points its abdomen into the wind, and collects the moisture that condenses on its body.

MOPPING UP

Before it can eat, a housefly must pour saliva over its food. The saliva often dries to form small spots that can be seen after the fly has moved on.

PATIENT KILLER

A praying mantis surprises its victims by striking out with its front legs. The legs snap shut and help grip the prey with sharp spines. The mantis often begins to feed even while its catch is still struggling to escape.

FEROCIOUS TWIG
Most caterpillars eat plants for food, but this looper moth caterpillar catches other insects. Camouflaged to look like a twig, it attacks small flies when they land nearby.

DEADLY DASH
After cockroaches, tiger beetles are among the fastest sprinters of the insect world. Moving at more than 1½ ft (0.5 m) per second, this tiger beetle is chasing some ants. The beetle's large jaws will quickly snatch and crush the ants.

Predators and Parasites

One third of all insects feed on other animals, either as predators or parasites. Predators catch their prey by hunting it actively, or lying in wait until food comes within reach. Some of the most spectacular hunters feed in the air. Dragonflies, for example, swoop down and snatch up other flying insects with their long legs. On the ground, active hunters include fast-moving beetles, as well as many ants and wasps. Some wasps specialize in hunting spiders, which they sting—sometimes after a fierce battle. Insects that hunt by stealth, or lying in wait, are usually harder to spot. These include mantises and bugs, which are often superbly camouflaged to match their background. A few of these stationary hunters build special traps to catch their food. Antlion larvae dig steep-sided pits in loose soil and wait for ants to tumble in. Insects that are parasites live on or inside another animal, called the host, and feed on its body or blood. The host animal can sometimes be harmed or killed.

EASY PICKINGS
Hunting is sometimes easy work. Because aphids move very slowly, they cannot escape hungry ladybugs.

UNDERWATER ATTACK
Only a few insects are large enough to kill vertebrates (animals with backbones). This diving beetle has managed to catch a salamander.

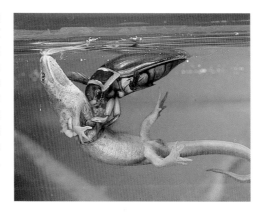

DEATH OF A BEE
Assassin bugs use their sharp beak to stab their victims and then suck out the body fluids. This one has caught a honeybee by lying in wait inside a flower.

CLEANING UP

Instead of hunting live animals, burying beetles feed on dead bodies. They bury carcasses, then feed themselves and their larvae on the remains.

DINING IN

Parasitic insects use living animals as fresh food. Many lay their eggs on the larvae of other insects, or inject eggs through the skin of the victim. When the eggs hatch, these larvae feed on their host. They start with the less essential parts of the host's body, so that it survives for as long as possible. Eventually, they burst out through the host's skin and turn into adults. This hawk moth caterpillar has been feasted on by parasitic wasps, and is covered with their empty cocoons.

DID YOU KNOW?

The larvae of fungus gnats, found in caves in New Zealand, catch flying insects by glowing in the dark. Each larva produces a thread of sticky mucus that traps insects as they fly towards the glowing light. The larva then eats the insect and the trap.

FLYING COURIER
Bees, butterflies, moths and wasps are all common visitors to flowers. These insects become dusted with pollen while they feed on the sugary nectar of the flowers.

Insects and Plants

When insects first appeared on Earth, they found a world brimming with plants. Over millions of years, insects and plants evolved side by side. During this time, some insects became deadly enemies of plants, but others became valuable partners in the struggle for survival. Insects use plants for many things, but the most important of all is for food. Different insects eat all parts of plants, from roots and stems to leaves and flowers. Most of them eat living plants, but some help to break down plants once they are dead. By doing this, insects help to recycle important nutrients so that other plants can use them. Insects also live on or in plants, and they often damage plants when they set up home. Despite this insect attack, plants are not completely defenseless. Many use sticky hairs or chemicals to keep insects away, and some even catch insects and digest them. However, not all visitors are unwelcome. When bees feed at flowers, they carry pollen from plant to plant. This helps plants to pollinate and spread to new areas.

GETTING A GRIP
Caterpillars have to hang on tight while they feed. They do this with special "legs" that end in sucker-like pads. They lose these legs when they become moths or butterflies.

BREAKING OUT
Seeds are packed with stores of food that help young plants to survive. This weevil climbing out of a grain of wheat has just finished eating some of these nutrients.

SLOW GROWTH
The larva of a stag beetle spends its entire early life hidden inside rotting wood. Because wood is not very nutritious, it takes the larva a long time to mature.

STRANGE BUT TRUE

The caterpillars of one Mexican moth grow inside the beans of a small bush. If a bean falls onto warm, sunny ground, the caterpillar inside jerks its body to make the bean "jump" into the shade. Each bean can move up to 2 in (5 cm) in a single hop.

18

LEAFY FEAST
Eating side by side, beetle larvae chew away at a leaf. Insects kill some plants, but enough plants are always left to allow both plants and insects to survive.

BUILDING WITH LEAVES
Female leafcutter bees clip out pieces of leaf with their jaws, and take the pieces back to their nests. They use them to make tube-shaped cells for larvae.

PLANTS THAT EAT INSECTS

In order to grow, plants need substances called mineral nutrients. They usually get these from the ground, but some plants that live where nutrients are scarce also get them from the bodies of insects. This sundew has trapped a fly in its sticky hairs, and will soon digest its prey. Other carnivorous plants catch insects in fluid-filled traps, or with leaves that suddenly snap shut.

19

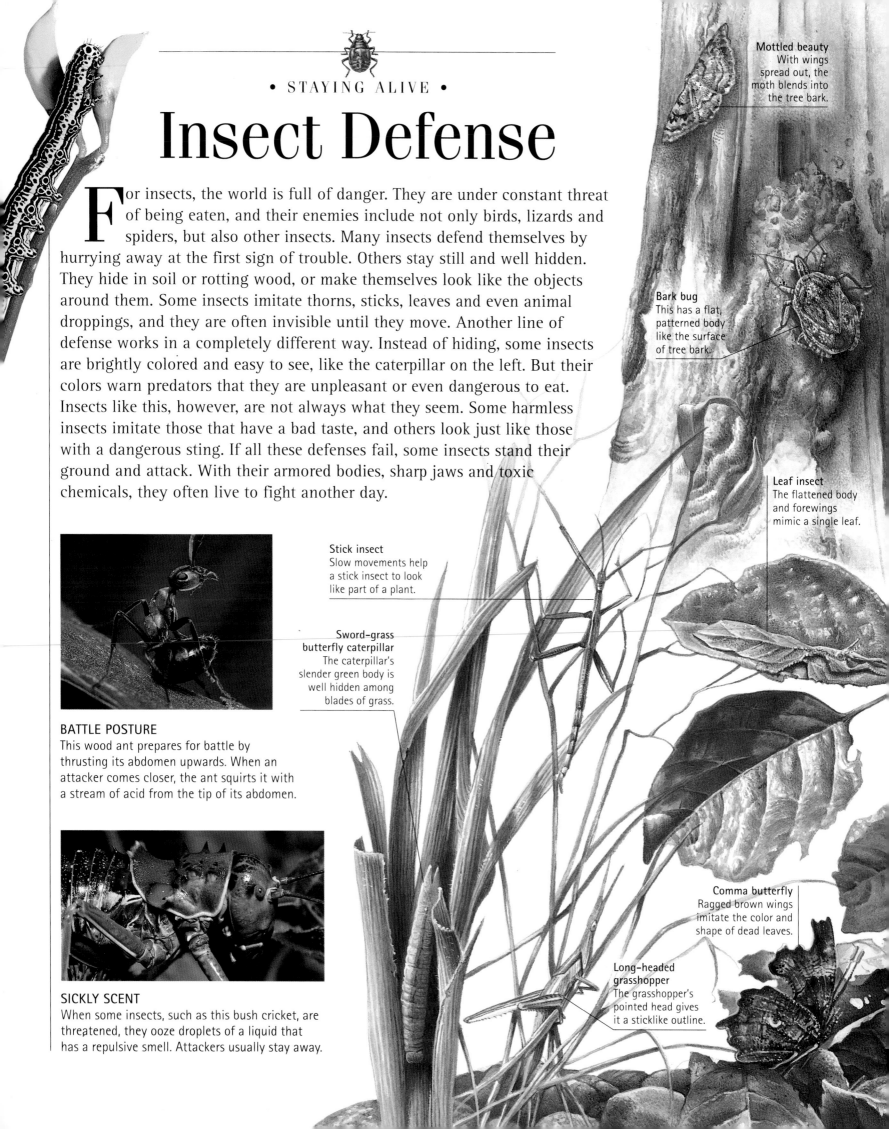

Insect Defense

For insects, the world is full of danger. They are under constant threat of being eaten, and their enemies include not only birds, lizards and spiders, but also other insects. Many insects defend themselves by hurrying away at the first sign of trouble. Others stay still and well hidden. They hide in soil or rotting wood, or make themselves look like the objects around them. Some insects imitate thorns, sticks, leaves and even animal droppings, and they are often invisible until they move. Another line of defense works in a completely different way. Instead of hiding, some insects are brightly colored and easy to see, like the caterpillar on the left. But their colors warn predators that they are unpleasant or even dangerous to eat. Insects like this, however, are not always what they seem. Some harmless insects imitate those that have a bad taste, and others look just like those with a dangerous sting. If all these defenses fail, some insects stand their ground and attack. With their armored bodies, sharp jaws and toxic chemicals, they often live to fight another day.

Mottled beauty
With wings spread out, the moth blends into the tree bark.

Bark bug
This has a flat, patterned body like the surface of tree bark.

Leaf insect
The flattened body and forewings mimic a single leaf.

Stick insect
Slow movements help a stick insect to look like part of a plant.

Sword-grass butterfly caterpillar
The caterpillar's slender green body is well hidden among blades of grass.

BATTLE POSTURE
This wood ant prepares for battle by thrusting its abdomen upwards. When an attacker comes closer, the ant squirts it with a stream of acid from the tip of its abdomen.

Comma butterfly
Ragged brown wings imitate the color and shape of dead leaves.

Long-headed grasshopper
The grasshopper's pointed head gives it a sticklike outline.

SICKLY SCENT
When some insects, such as this bush cricket, are threatened, they ooze droplets of a liquid that has a repulsive smell. Attackers usually stay away.

BLENDING IN

Insects are experts in the art of camouflage. This scene shows how 13 different insects use camouflage to avoid being spotted.

STARING EYES

Many moths have two large spots on their back wings. When disturbed, they reveal the spots, which look like two eyes set in a menacing face.

STRANGE BUT TRUE

It is hard to imagine an insect imitating a snake, but this is how some swallowtail caterpillars defend themselves. On their back, they have two large eyespots, which make them look like a small poisonous snake.

Emerald moth caterpillar
The body projections make this caterpillar look like a twig with buds.

Swallowtail butterfly larva
The texture and shape of the larva's body look like bird droppings.

Bush cricket
The veined front wings are pressed together to look like an upright leaf.

DEFENSE PLANS

There is no such thing as one completely successful defense plan. Many insects have several ways to defend themselves. If one method is not successful, they will try another. The puss moth caterpillar relies initially on camouflage, but if an attacker sees it, the caterpillar moves onto the next plan. This involves inflating its head, and producing a pair of "horns" to frighten its attacker. If the caterpillar is still in danger, it squirts a spray of acid at its attacker, from a gland just beneath the head.

Flower mantis
This mantis is the same color as the flower. It is disguised as it waits to catch prey.

Angle shades moth
The wings look like a newly fallen leaf.

Cryptic grasshopper
The round outline and mottled colors imitate a small pebble.

KICKING BACK

The giant weta from New Zealand raises its powerful back legs to show that it can fight back. These legs have large spines.

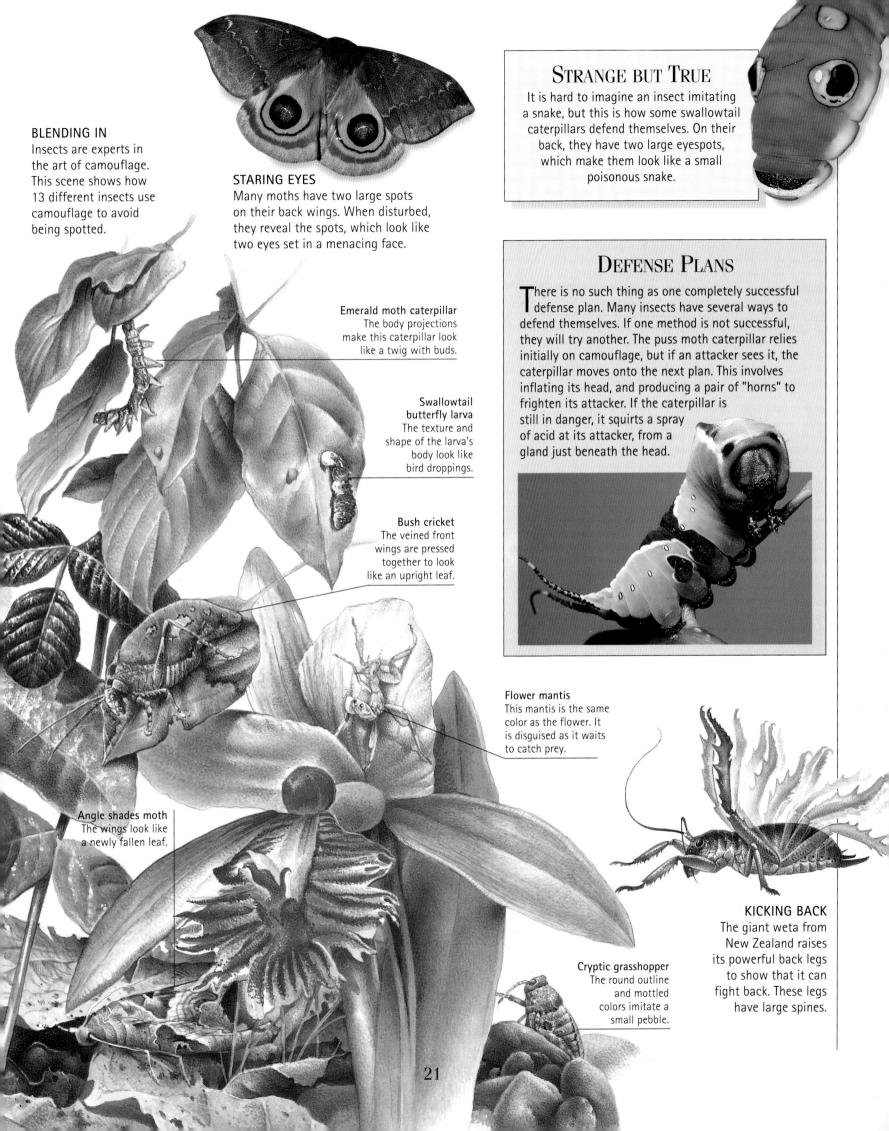

Getting Started

DANGEROUS MOMENT
Male insects are often smaller than females, and some have to be careful when they mate. Unless he is careful, this male mantis will end up as a meal for his partner.

FOOD FOR THE YOUNG
Insects often use their sense of smell to find good places for their eggs. This dead mouse has attracted blowflies that are ready to lay eggs.

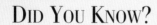

Animals begin life in two different ways. Some develop inside their mother's body until they are ready to be born. Others, including most insects, develop from eggs outside their mother's body. Before a female insect can lay her eggs, she normally has to mate. Once this has happened, she chooses a place for her eggs, making sure that each one is near a source of suitable food. In most cases, she then abandons them, and makes no attempt to look after her young. However, not all insects start life this way. A few female insects can reproduce without needing to mate. Some insects give birth to live young, such as aphids who give birth to nymphs, and tsetse flies who give birth to larvae. A few insects are careful parents and take care of their eggs. Female earwigs lay small clutches of eggs and look after them by licking them clean. Many bugs carry their eggs on their backs, and guard their young after they hatch.

A QUEEN'S LIFE
In an ant colony, only one individual—the queen—lays eggs. The eggs are carried away by worker ants, who tend and feed the young after they hatch. Most termites also reproduce this way.

DID YOU KNOW?
Insects that give birth to live young have fast-growing families. Within a few days, a female leaf beetle or aphid can be surrounded by dozens of offspring. Unlike insects that start life as eggs, each one can feed right away.

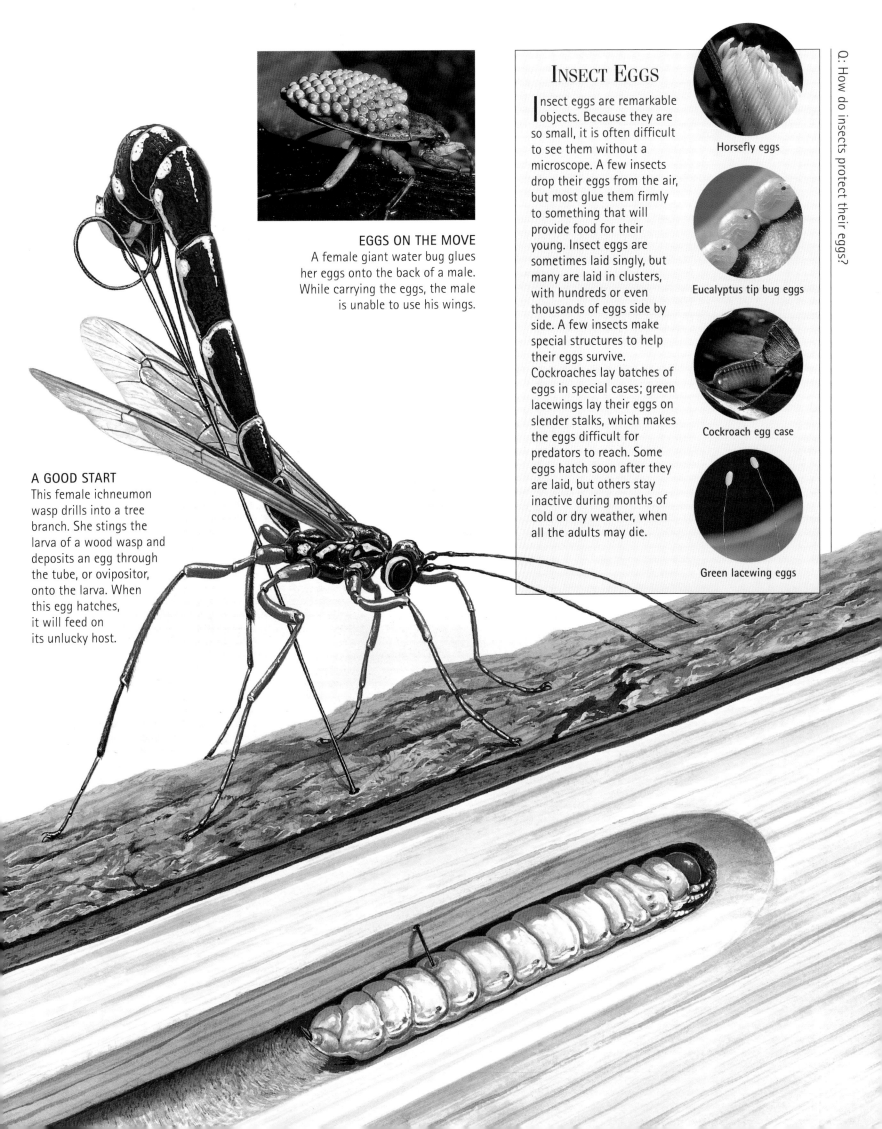

EGGS ON THE MOVE
A female giant water bug glues her eggs onto the back of a male. While carrying the eggs, the male is unable to use his wings.

INSECT EGGS

Insect eggs are remarkable objects. Because they are so small, it is often difficult to see them without a microscope. A few insects drop their eggs from the air, but most glue them firmly to something that will provide food for their young. Insect eggs are sometimes laid singly, but many are laid in clusters, with hundreds or even thousands of eggs side by side. A few insects make special structures to help their eggs survive. Cockroaches lay batches of eggs in special cases; green lacewings lay their eggs on slender stalks, which makes the eggs difficult for predators to reach. Some eggs hatch soon after they are laid, but others stay inactive during months of cold or dry weather, when all the adults may die.

Horsefly eggs

Eucalyptus tip bug eggs

Cockroach egg case

Green lacewing eggs

A GOOD START
This female ichneumon wasp drills into a tree branch. She stings the larva of a wood wasp and deposits an egg through the tube, or ovipositor, onto the larva. When this egg hatches, it will feed on its unlucky host.

From Nymph to Adult

After an insect has hatched out of its egg, it starts to feed and grow. However, as well as growing, it often changes shape. This is called metamorphosis. In some insects, the changes are only slight, so the young insect looks much like the adult form. In others, the changes are so great that the young and adult look completely different. Insects that change only slightly include dragonflies, grasshoppers, earwigs, cockroaches, true bugs and praying mantises. Their young are called nymphs. A nymph does not have wings, although it does have small wing buds, and it is usually a different color from its parents. It often lives in a different habitat and feeds on different food. Most nymphs will molt several times. Each time a nymph sheds its skin, its body gets bigger and its wing buds become longer. Eventually, the nymph is ready for its final molt. It breaks out of its old skin, and emerges as an adult insect with working wings. It can then fly away to find a mate.

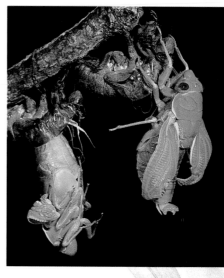

FINAL MOLT
After many years feeding underground as nymphs, these cicadas are shedding their skins for the last time. Their crumpled wings will soon expand and dry.

UNDERWATER NYMPHS
Adult dragonflies live in the air, but their nymphs develop under the water. Each nymph lives in water for up to five years before it hauls itself up a plant stem, sheds its skin for the last time, and emerges as an adult, able to fly.

MANTIS MARCH
These newly hatched praying mantis nymphs look like miniature versions of their parents. They have well-developed legs, but their wing buds are still very small.

Laying eggs
This dragonfly inserts her eggs into a water plant. Some species let the eggs fall to the bottom of ponds.

On the move
Dragonfly eggs can take several weeks to hatch. Each tiny nymph chews its way out of its egg case.

Box elder bug

Desert locust

Earwig

NYMPH TO ADULT
Like their parents (far right), nymphs have six legs. Their bodies change in proportion as they grow, but they keep the same overall shape.

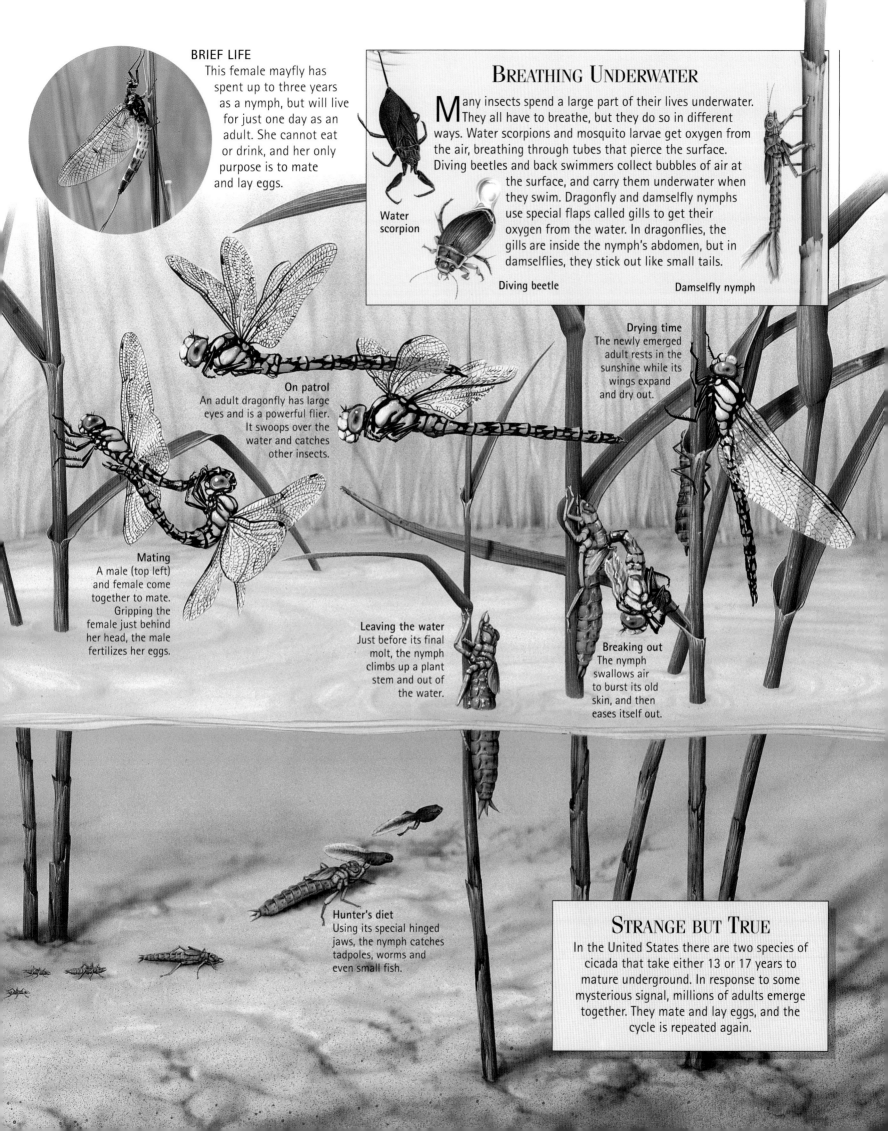

BRIEF LIFE
This female mayfly has spent up to three years as a nymph, but will live for just one day as an adult. She cannot eat or drink, and her only purpose is to mate and lay eggs.

BREATHING UNDERWATER

Many insects spend a large part of their lives underwater. They all have to breathe, but they do so in different ways. Water scorpions and mosquito larvae get oxygen from the air, breathing through tubes that pierce the surface. Diving beetles and back swimmers collect bubbles of air at the surface, and carry them underwater when they swim. Dragonfly and damselfly nymphs use special flaps called gills to get their oxygen from the water. In dragonflies, the gills are inside the nymph's abdomen, but in damselflies, they stick out like small tails.

Water scorpion

Diving beetle

Damselfly nymph

On patrol
An adult dragonfly has large eyes and is a powerful flier. It swoops over the water and catches other insects.

Mating
A male (top left) and female come together to mate. Gripping the female just behind her head, the male fertilizes her eggs.

Drying time
The newly emerged adult rests in the sunshine while its wings expand and dry out.

Leaving the water
Just before its final molt, the nymph climbs up a plant stem and out of the water.

Breaking out
The nymph swallows air to burst its old skin, and then eases itself out.

Hunter's diet
Using its special hinged jaws, the nymph catches tadpoles, worms and even small fish.

STRANGE BUT TRUE

In the United States there are two species of cicada that take either 13 or 17 years to mature underground. In response to some mysterious signal, millions of adults emerge together. They mate and lay eggs, and the cycle is repeated again.

A CHANGE OF LIFE
The atlas moth has four stages in its life cycle—egg, larva, pupa and adult. Larvae put all their energy into feeding, while adults mate and lay eggs.

Mating
A female's scent attracts a male, and the moths mate.

The next stage
A larva, or caterpillar, hatches from an egg. It grows bigger with several molts.

Laying eggs
The female moth searches for suitable food plants and glues her eggs to the leaves.

DID YOU KNOW?
Most larvae feed for many hours every day, and they put on weight very quickly. Just before they turn into pupae, fully grown larvae are often heavier than the adult insects of the same species.

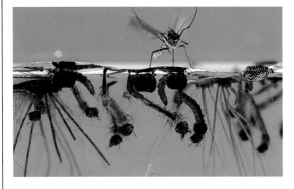

LEGLESS LARVAE
Mosquito larvae live in water and feed on microscopic animals. They swim by wriggling their bodies, and breathe through short tubes.

• CYCLES OF LIFE •

A Complete Change

Many young insects look quite unlike their parents. They do not have wings, and some do not even have legs. They often spend all their time on, or in, the things they eat. Young insects such as these are called larvae, and they include maggots, grubs and caterpillars. Compared to adult insects, they have soft bodies. Larvae protect themselves by tasting horrible, by being difficult to swallow, or by hiding away. A typical larva feeds for several weeks, shedding its skin several times while growing. When mature, its appetite suddenly vanishes, it stops moving and it becomes a pupa. The pupa has a tough outer case, and is sometimes protected by a silk cocoon. Inside the case, the larva's body changes dramatically. It is broken down and reassembled, so that it gradually turns into an adult insect. When this change, or metamorphosis, is complete, the case splits open and the adult insect, with wings, breaks out. It is now ready to reproduce.

26

Pupating
The caterpillar fastens itself in position with threads of silk.

Opening up
After breaking open the pupal case, the adult moth pumps blood into its wings.

Airborne
When its wing veins have hardened, the moth flies off.

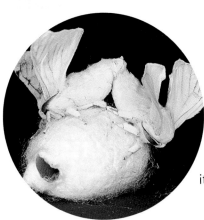

NATURAL SILK
Each silk moth cocoon is made of a single silk thread more than 1/2 mile (1 km) long. As soon as a moth emerges from its cocoon, it mates.

PAMPERED UPBRINGING
Honeybee larvae mature inside wax cells, and worker bees bring food to them. These bees are turning into pupae, and will soon emerge as adults.

TIME FOR A CHANGE

Insects that change completely when they mature have four stages in their life cycles. Each stage usually lasts for a different length of time and these times vary from species to species. The stag beetle is a relatively slow developer, and spends many months as a larva hidden in wood, feeding only on rotting vegetation. The ladybug develops more quickly, and spends over half its life as an adult. The northern caddis fly spends most of its life as a larva. It lives in ponds and quiet waters in a specially constructed case.

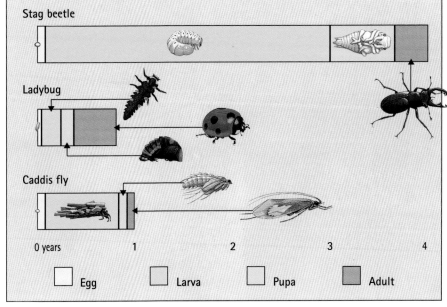

Stag beetle

Ladybug

Caddis fly

0 years   1   2   3   4

☐ Egg   ☐ Larva   ☐ Pupa   ■ Adult

Discover more in The Great Success Story

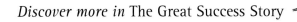

27

Insect Flight

Insects were the first animals to fly. Today they share the air with birds and bats, but they are still the most numerous fliers in the animal world. Some insects fly on their own. Others, such as midges and locusts, gather in swarms. A swarm can contain just a few dozen insects, or more than a billion. Flying allows insects to escape from danger, and makes it easier for them to find mates. It is also a perfect way to reach food. Bees and butterflies fly among flowers, and hawk moths often hover in front of them. Dragonflies use flight to attack other insects in the air. They are the fastest fliers in the insect world, and can reach speeds of more than 31 miles (50 km) per hour. Most insects have two pairs of wings, made of the same material that covers the rest of their bodies. The wings are powered by muscles in the thorax. These muscles either flap the wings directly, or make the thorax move and this causes the wings to flap.

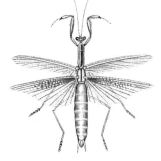

WINGS COMPARED
In most insects, the front and back wings look different. Insect wings are supported by branching veins, and are sometimes covered with tiny hairs or scales.

Pleated back wings
The back wings of a mantis fold up like fans when not in use.

DID YOU KNOW?
Insects such as thrips and aphids are too small and slow to make much headway on their own. Instead, they are carried by the wind, blowing them from one place to another far away.

VERTICAL TAKEOFF
Butterflies rest with their wings together. At takeoff, the wings peel apart, and the air sucks the butterfly upwards and away from danger.

REFUELING STOP
Flight is a fast and efficient way of getting about, but it uses a lot of energy. Many insects, such as bees, drink sugary nectar from flowers to give them energy.

LONG-DISTANCE TRAVELERS

Although insects are small animals, some of them travel huge distances in search of food or warmth. Dragonflies, locusts and moths often migrate, but the star travelers of the insect world are butterflies. In spring, North American monarch butterflies (left) set off northwards from Mexico. Many travel more than 1,500 miles (2,400 km). Painted lady butterflies set out from North Africa, and often make even longer journeys. Some of them manage to cross the Arctic Circle in Scandinavia, making a total distance of more than 1,800 miles (2,900 km).

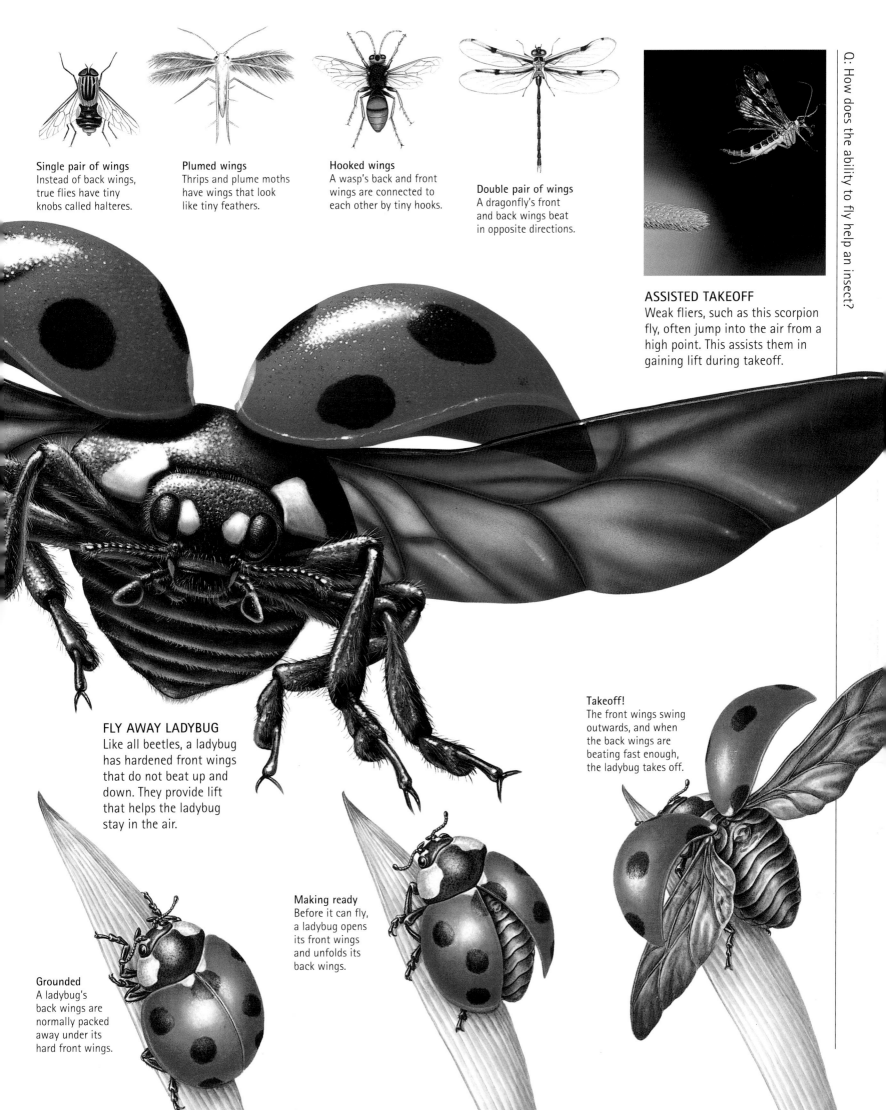

Single pair of wings
Instead of back wings, true flies have tiny knobs called halteres.

Plumed wings
Thrips and plume moths have wings that look like tiny feathers.

Hooked wings
A wasp's back and front wings are connected to each other by tiny hooks.

Double pair of wings
A dragonfly's front and back wings beat in opposite directions.

ASSISTED TAKEOFF
Weak fliers, such as this scorpion fly, often jump into the air from a high point. This assists them in gaining lift during takeoff.

FLY AWAY LADYBUG
Like all beetles, a ladybug has hardened front wings that do not beat up and down. They provide lift that helps the ladybug stay in the air.

Takeoff!
The front wings swing outwards, and when the back wings are beating fast enough, the ladybug takes off.

Making ready
Before it can fly, a ladybug opens its front wings and unfolds its back wings.

Grounded
A ladybug's back wings are normally packed away under its hard front wings.

LOOPING WALK
Some caterpillars move by holding the ground tight with their front legs, and pulling their body into a loop. They stretch forwards to straighten the loop, and then start the process again.

• AN INSECT'S WORLD •

Moving Around

HEAD-BANGER
A click beetle escapes danger by lying on its back and keeping perfectly still (above left). If attacked its head suddenly snaps upwards, hurling it out of harm's way and back onto its feet.

Many people find insects alarming because of their sudden movements. Insects are not always fast, but because they weigh so little, most of them can stop and start far more suddenly than we can. The way an insect moves depends on where it lives. On land, the slowest movers are legless larvae. They have to wriggle to get around. Adult insects normally move using their legs, and they either walk or run, or jump into the air. The champion jumpers of the insect world are grasshoppers and crickets, but jumping insects also include fleas, froghoppers and some beetles. Tiny, wingless insects called springtails also jump, but instead of using their legs, they launch themselves by flicking a special "tail." Legs are useful in water, and insects have evolved a variety of leg shapes to suit watery ways of life. Water boatmen and diving beetles have legs like oars, and row their way through the water. Pond-skaters live on top of the water, and have long and slender legs that spread their weight over the surface.

WALKING IN THREES
Insects walk by moving three legs at a time—one on one side, and two on the other. This makes their bodies zigzag as they move along.

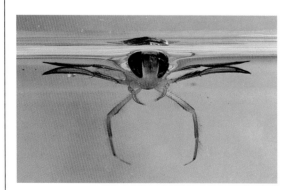

ROWING ALONG
The lesser water boatman has flattened back legs fringed with hairs. It uses these to push itself along. This species swims right side up, but some water boatmen swim upside down.

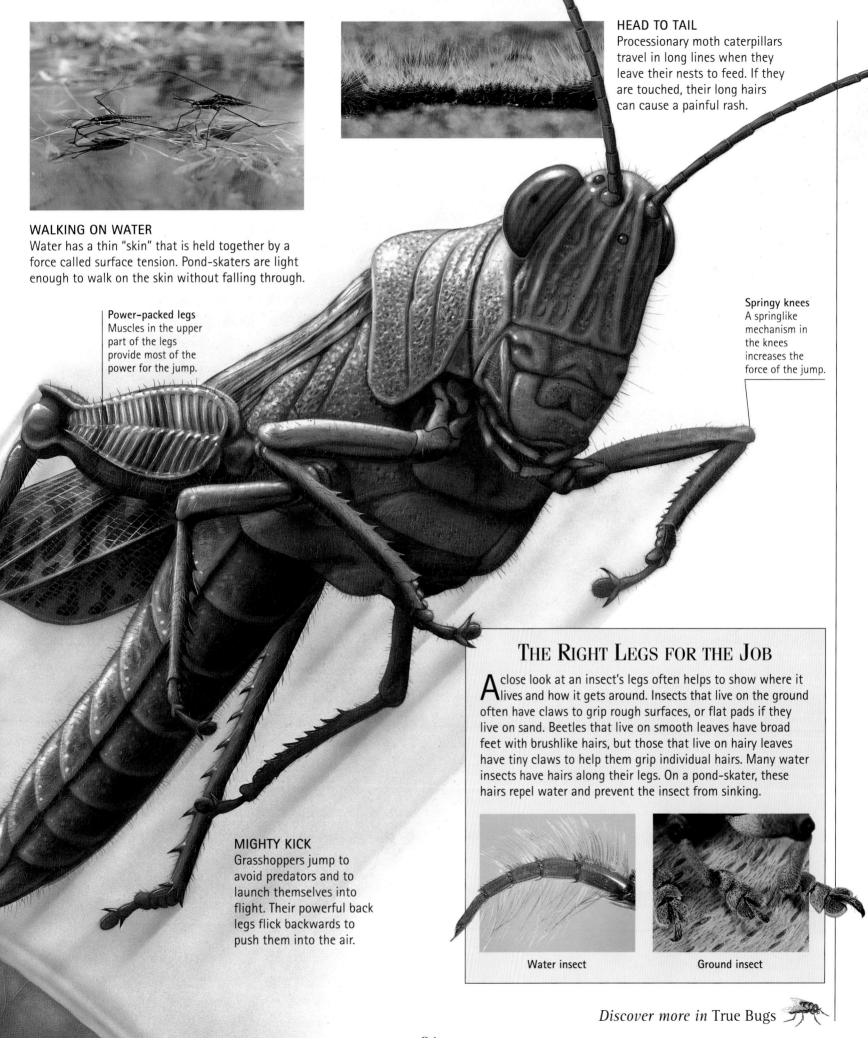

WALKING ON WATER
Water has a thin "skin" that is held together by a force called surface tension. Pond-skaters are light enough to walk on the skin without falling through.

HEAD TO TAIL
Processionary moth caterpillars travel in long lines when they leave their nests to feed. If they are touched, their long hairs can cause a painful rash.

Power-packed legs
Muscles in the upper part of the legs provide most of the power for the jump.

Springy knees
A springlike mechanism in the knees increases the force of the jump.

MIGHTY KICK
Grasshoppers jump to avoid predators and to launch themselves into flight. Their powerful back legs flick backwards to push them into the air.

THE RIGHT LEGS FOR THE JOB

A close look at an insect's legs often helps to show where it lives and how it gets around. Insects that live on the ground often have claws to grip rough surfaces, or flat pads if they live on sand. Beetles that live on smooth leaves have broad feet with brushlike hairs, but those that live on hairy leaves have tiny claws to help them grip individual hairs. Many water insects have hairs along their legs. On a pond-skater, these hairs repel water and prevent the insect from sinking.

Water insect

Ground insect

Discover more in True Bugs

Making Contact

In every insect's life, there are times when it has to make contact with other members of its species. It may need to warn of danger, to attract a mate, or to prove that it is not an enemy but a friend. Many insects communicate by sight, and they often use bright colors or patterns to identify themselves. After dark, most insects are hard to see, but fireflies are easy to spot. They make their own light, and flash coded signals to one another through the dark. For crickets, cicadas and some smaller insects, sound provides a way to contact a mate. Unlike sight, sound works during the day and night, and allows an insect to stay hidden while it broadcasts its call. Insects often use touch and taste to communicate when they meet, but they can also make contact by smell. Some of their scents waft a long way through the air, while others mark the ground to show where they have been.

Male firefly

LIGHTS IN THE NIGHT
Fireflies are small beetles that make contact using a pale-greenish light. The males flash as they fly overhead and the females—which are often wingless—flash back from the ground.

Female firefly

THE HONEYBEE DANCE

When a worker honeybee finds a good food source, it returns to the hive to pass on the news. It tells the other honeybees the distance and location of the food through a special figure eight dance. If the food is far away from the hive, the honeybee does a waggle in the middle of the figure eight (as shown below). The speed of the waggle tells the honeybees how far they must fly to find the food. The angle of the waggle shows the honeybees where the food is in relation to the sun.

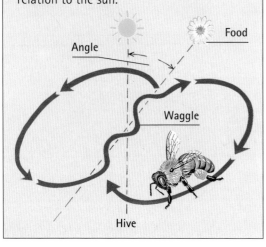

Angle

Food

Waggle

Hive

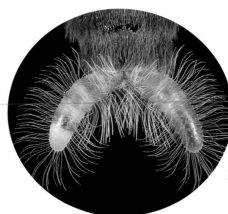

SCENTED MOTH
The male tiger moth attracts females by a scent called a pheromone, which is released into the air by two glands in the abdomen. These fold away when not in use.

SOUND SIGNALS
A grasshopper calls by scraping its back legs against the hard edges of its front wings. This causes the wings to vibrate and make a sound. This process is called stridulation.

TOUCH AND TASTE
When two ants meet, they touch each other briefly with their antennae. This tells them if they are from the same nest, and passes on the taste of any food they have found.

DID YOU KNOW?

The male mole cricket attracts mates with one of the loudest calls in the insect world. The cricket makes his call by rubbing his front wings together, and his Y-shaped burrow amplifies the sound. In still air, it can be heard more than 1/2 mile (800 m) away.

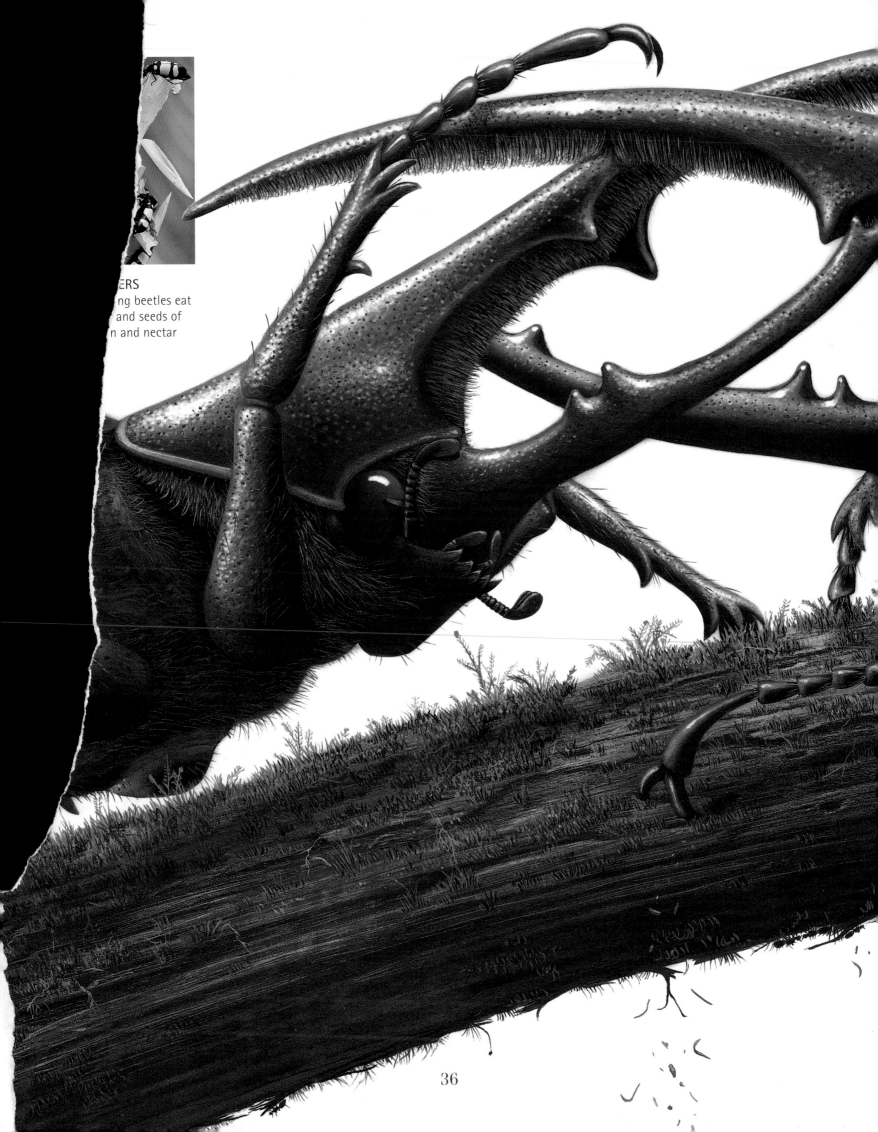

ERS
ng beetles eat
and seeds of
n and nectar

BIZARRE BEETLES

Over millions of years, many beetles have evolved strange shapes to suit their way of life. Some shapes are easy to explain, but many are still a mystery.

Giraffe weevil
A tapering thorax and long head may help this beetle to feed.

Tortoise beetle
Its rounded front wings and flat thorax make the tortoise beetle look like a coin.

Long-horned beetle
Like the related harlequin, this beetle has long "horns" that are actually antennae.

Harlequin beetle
This brilliantly colored tropical beetle lives in fig trees, and feeds at night.

Violin beetle
Two transparent flaps flank this beetle's abdomen. It lives between layers of bracket fungi.

Weevil
This beetle, which feeds on plants, has a long snout with jaws at its tip.

Beetles

There are more species of beetle in the world than any other kind of animal. More than 400,000 different kinds are estimated, and more are discovered each year. Beetles live in a wide range of habitats, and they vary immensely in size. The heaviest is the goliath beetle from Africa, but the largest is the male hercules beetle from Central America, which can be more than 7½ in (19 cm) long. The smallest, known as a feather-winged beetle, looks like a tiny dot and is only just visible to the naked eye. Despite their differences in size, beetles have one important feature in common—the hard, rigid front wings that fit over the back wings like a case. This prevents the back wings from being damaged, and allows beetles to clamber about in search of food. Many beetles are vegetarians, but others are hunters that feed on other animals. A few rummage their way through leaf litter, and live by eating the remains of decaying animals.

LOCKING HORNS

Male hercules beetles use their horns to grapple with rivals. Although these fights look ferocious, they rarely produce lasting injuries, and the loser usually runs away.

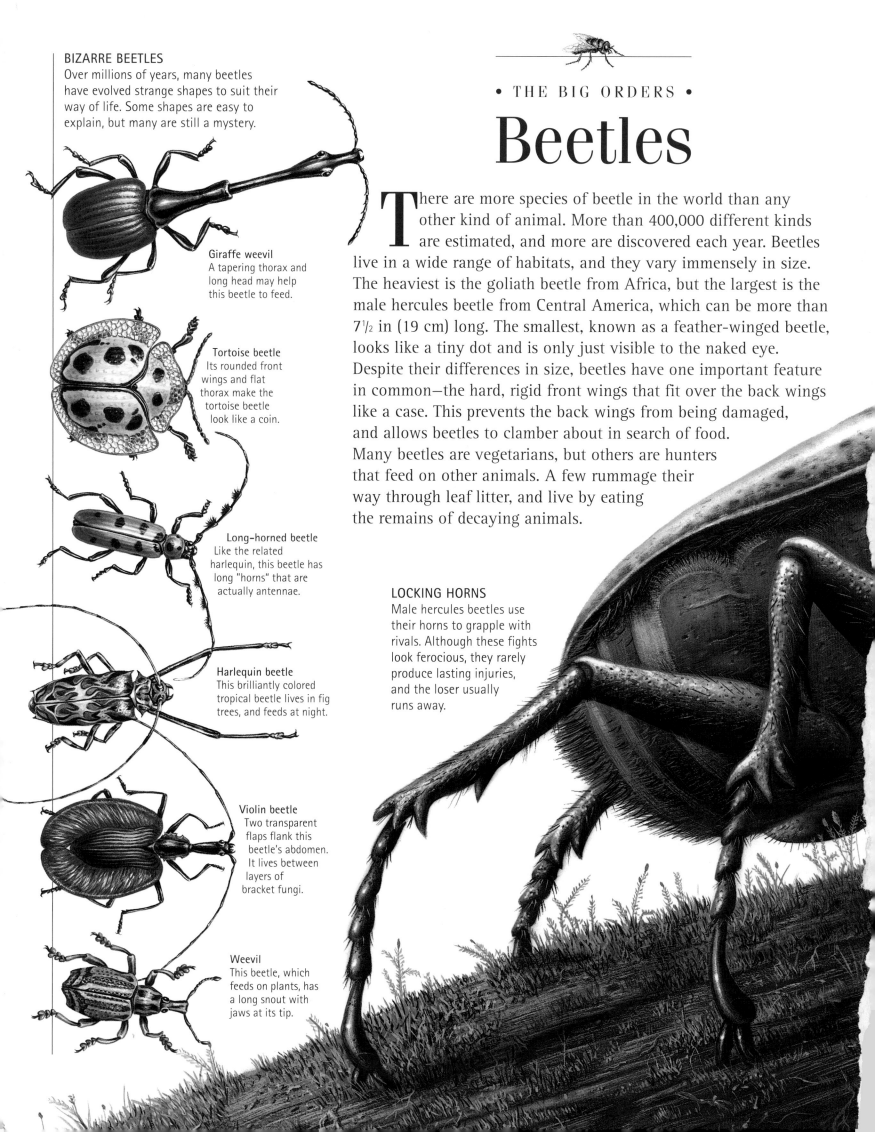

Nests and Shelters

Which animals build the most elaborate homes in the living world? The answer is not mammals or birds, but insects. Insects are among the most experienced of nature's builders, and they make many different kinds of structures. Some insects work on their own and build simple shelters just for themselves or for their young. Others—the termites, ants, social bees and wasps—work in family groups. Their nests are far more ambitious, and are big enough to house thousands or even millions of individuals. These social insects use a range of building materials, from leaves and dead plants to wood fibers, mud and wax. They often chew up the material to form a paste. They then spread the paste where it is needed. In their mammoth building operations, no animal is in charge. The builders are guided by instinct, and each knows exactly what to do.

ONE FOR THE POT
A female potter wasp makes a hollow pot out of mud. Inside it, she puts a caterpillar that she has killed, and lays an egg on it. She seals the pot, and after the grub hatches, it eats the caterpillar.

SNUG AND DRY
Termites build nests on the ground and also high in trees. This nest from West Africa has sloping roofs to shed heavy rain.

Hard walls
Soft mud dries in the sun to create hard, porous walls.

STRANGE BUT TRUE
Young froghopper bugs feed on plant sap, and they often protect themselves by making a "home" of frothy bubbles. The bubbles hide the bugs away from birds, and also from many of their insect enemies.

Butterflies and Moths

COLORED SCALES
The scales on a butterfly's wings overlap like tiles on a roof. They often reflect light in a special way that produces brilliant colors.

Butterflies are the most eye-catching members of the insect world, while moths are often quite dull. Yet despite their differences in color, these insects are closely related and have many features in common.

Butterflies and moths spend the first part of their lives as caterpillars. They change shape during a resting stage as a pupa (left), and emerge as adults with wings covered with tiny scales. Unlike caterpillars, an adult butterfly or moth eats liquid food, such as nectar or rotting fruit. It does this with a sucking tube called a proboscis, which coils up when the insect is not using it. Butterflies fly by day, but most moths fly at dusk or after dark, and spend the day hidden on leaves or trees. There are more than 150,000 species of butterfly and moth. The largest have wingspans of more than 10 in (25 cm), but the smallest, called pygmy moths, are not much bigger than a fingernail.

I SPY
Most moths use camouflage to protect them during the day. When this moth from Borneo rests on a tree, it seems to disappear.

Hercules moth caterpillar

Orchard butterfly caterpillar

SURVIVAL KIT
Caterpillars have many enemies, so they defend themselves with poisonous chemicals, irritating hairs, and inflatable "horns" that release an unpleasant smell.

Silk moth caterpillar

FLY-BY-NIGHTS

Many night-time insects are attracted to bright lights. They flutter around street lights, and often gather outside windows after dark. Scientists are not certain why light attracts insects in this way, although with moths, it may be that the light disrupts their navigation system. Moths probably fly in straight lines by using a distant light, such as the moon, like a fixed point on a compass. When a moth does this with a nearby light, the system does not work, because the position of the "fixed" point changes as soon as the moth flies past. As a result, the moth spirals around the light, and eventually flies into it.

CIRCLES ON WATER
Whirligig beetles live on the surface of ponds and streams. They judge the direction of food and avoid obstacles by creating ripples, and sensing how these bounce back.

HIDE-AND-SEEK
Some beetles use camouflage to avoid being seen. These beetles from Madagascar, look like the lichen on this lichen-covered twig.

Some beetle larvae feed on wood and often take many years to mature. In a house in England, a beetle emerged from a wooden staircase 47 years after the timber had been cut and used to build the stairs.

WINNER TAKES ALL
Female hercules beetles have no horns. Here, a female waits while two males fight for the right to mate with her.

BURROWING UNDER BARK

Bark beetles develop beneath tree bark, where the wood is full of nutritious sap. The female beetle excavates a tunnel parallel to the surface and lays her eggs at intervals along it. When the larvae hatch, they burrow sideways, making tunnels of their own. The result is a complex pattern of burrows that varies from one species to another. These tunnels are easy to see when a tree dies, and its bark falls away.

Five-spotted ladybug

Ten-spotted ladybug

VISUAL WARNING
The bright colors of ladybug beetles warn enemies that they have a bitter taste. The spots of each species are arranged in a different pattern.

Discover more in Insects and Plants

38

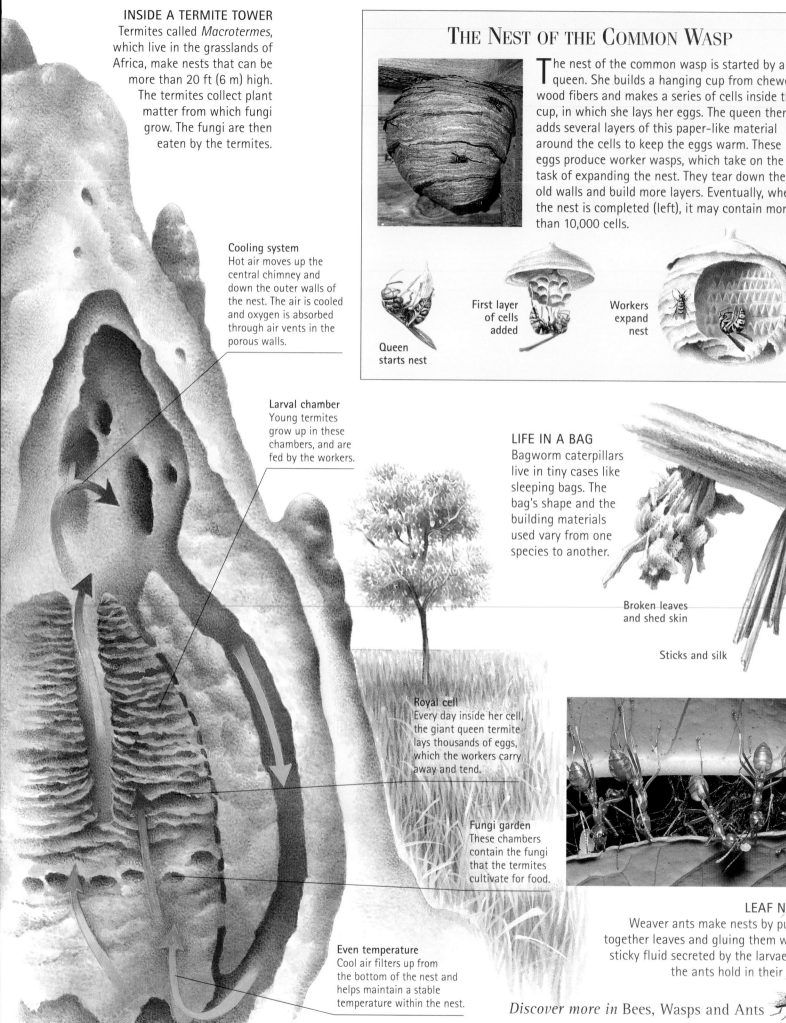

INSIDE A TERMITE TOWER
Termites called *Macrotermes*, which live in the grasslands of Africa, make nests that can be more than 20 ft (6 m) high. The termites collect plant matter from which fungi grow. The fungi are then eaten by the termites.

Cooling system
Hot air moves up the central chimney and down the outer walls of the nest. The air is cooled and oxygen is absorbed through air vents in the porous walls.

Larval chamber
Young termites grow up in these chambers, and are fed by the workers.

Royal cell
Every day inside her cell, the giant queen termite lays thousands of eggs, which the workers carry away and tend.

Fungi garden
These chambers contain the fungi that the termites cultivate for food.

Even temperature
Cool air filters up from the bottom of the nest and helps maintain a stable temperature within the nest.

THE NEST OF THE COMMON WASP

The nest of the common wasp is started by a queen. She builds a hanging cup from chewed wood fibers and makes a series of cells inside the cup, in which she lays her eggs. The queen then adds several layers of this paper-like material around the cells to keep the eggs warm. These eggs produce worker wasps, which take on the task of expanding the nest. They tear down the old walls and build more layers. Eventually, when the nest is completed (left), it may contain more than 10,000 cells.

Queen starts nest

First layer of cells added

Workers expand nest

LIFE IN A BAG
Bagworm caterpillars live in tiny cases like sleeping bags. The bag's shape and the building materials used vary from one species to another.

Broken leaves and shed skin

Sticks and silk

LEAF NESTS
Weaver ants make nests by pulling together leaves and gluing them with a sticky fluid secreted by the larvae that the ants hold in their jaws.

Discover more in Bees, Wasps and Ants

TWIN TAILS
Swallowtails get their name from the long "tail" on each back wing. These large butterflies are fast and powerful fliers.

Q: What are some of the differences between moths and butterflies?

Malaysian lacewing
butterfly

TIME OUT
Butterflies usually rest with their wings upright, although they often spread them when they bask in the sunshine. Moths usually rest with their wings held flat.

Yellow emperor
moth

BUTTERFLY OR MOTH?
Moths do not have a knob on the end of each antenna like most butterflies do. This elephant hawk moth has feathery antennae.

STRANGE BUT TRUE
Tear moths, from Southeast Asia, feed on the tears of large animals, such as cattle and buffaloes. Settling close to the eye, the moth drinks the tears through its long proboscis. Although they can be annoying, the moths do little harm.

Discover more in A Complete Change

41

Bees, Wasps and Ants

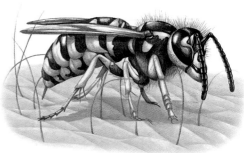

Most insects live alone, coming together only to mate, but social insects have a very different way of life. They live in family groups and share the work necessary to survive. Social insects include all ants and termites, and many species of bee and wasp. These insects usually build nests in which they raise their young and store food. Some nests contain fewer than a dozen insects, but others can house more than a million. Inside each nest, one insect—the queen—normally lays eggs, and all the other insects are her offspring. Workers look after the eggs, find food and raise the young, and in ant and termite colonies, soldiers defend the nest against attack. Every year, some of the males and queens fly away and mate. After mating, the male dies and the queen starts building a new nest. She is soon surrounded by a growing family of her own.

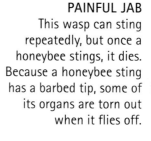

SOLITARY BEE
Not all bees live together. Most live a solitary life, such as this digger bee, digging its way to an underground nest.

Pollen stores

Drone
Drones are male bees that develop from unfertilized eggs. Their only job is to mate with new queens.

MAMMOTH LOAD
Leafcutter ants bite off pieces of plants, and carry them underground. Instead of eating these plant pieces, they eat the fungi that break the plants down.

Empty cell

Drone cell
Drone pupae need larger cells than worker pupae.

Queen cell
Larvae selected to become queens are fed only royal jelly and are raised in special cells.

Open larva cell
This cell contains a newly hatched larva. Larvae are first fed royal jelly, and later pollen and honey.

DID YOU KNOW?
Bumblebees survive as far north as the polar tundra, where the summers are cool and short. Their large bodies are covered with a layer of insulating hairs, and they insulate their nests to keep their larvae warm.

HIVE OF ACTIVITY
Honeybees collect nectar and pollen from flowers, and take them back to their nests made of wax. The bees use the wax cells for raising young and storing pollen and honey.

SAFETY IN NUMBERS
South American army ants march across the forest floor, preying on any small animals in their path.

LIVING FOOD STORES

Honey ants live in dry places, where flowers bloom for just a few weeks each year. To survive the long dry season, they store food and water in a remarkable way. Some of the workers collect sugary nectar and feed it to workers that remain underground. The abdomens of these workers swell up like balloons as they fill with nectar. Enough is stored to provide the whole nest with food and water in times of drought, until the rains return and flowers bloom once more.

Honey stores
The nectar is capped with wax and the bees change it into honey.

Nectar stores

Worker
Workers are females that cannot breed. Royal jelly is produced from glands in their head.

Queen bee
A queen can live for five years, and lays up to 1,500 eggs each day.

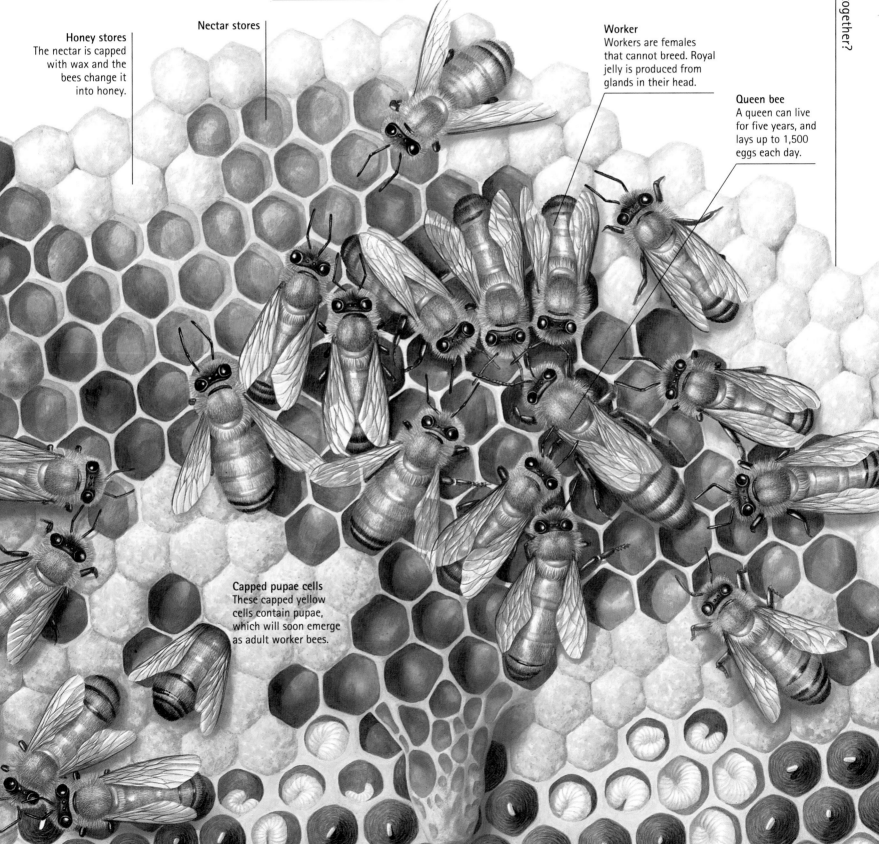

Capped pupae cells
These capped yellow cells contain pupae, which will soon emerge as adult worker bees.

QUESTION OF SIZE
Male stalk-eyed flies use their strange eyestalks to measure each other's size. The largest male wins the right to mate with females.

Flies

Flies are the aviation experts of the insect world. Unlike almost all other flying insects, they have only a single pair of wings, which gives them great speed and agility in the air. They also have excellent eyesight, and a pair of special stabilizers, called halteres. These keep them balanced while on the move. Altogether, there are 120,000 known species of fly. They include not only the flies that sometimes find their way indoors, but also midges and mosquitoes, brightly colored hover flies, and many other insects that buzz noisily through the air. Although all flies eat liquid food, they do so in different ways. Some mop up fluids from flowers and fruit, or from rotting remains. Others settle on skin and use their sharp mouthparts to collect a meal of blood. Flies begin life as legless larvae, which often live inside decomposing food.

LITTLE AND LARGE
The fruit fly (left) starts life as an egg, and matures in rotting fruit. The flesh fly facing it is born live, and lives in rotting meat.

BALANCING ACT
Flies have special balancing organs called halteres, which are the modified remnants of back wings. When a crane fly lands, its halteres are easy to see.

Haltere

UPSIDE DOWN

How do houseflies land on ceilings? By using high-speed photography, scientists have learned that they do it front-feet first. When a fly is about to land, it flies the right way up, but lifts its front legs above its body. The pads on its feet secrete an adhesive fluid, and the claws on its feet catch hold of the ceiling. The fly's body then flips upside down. Its other four legs make contact with the surface, and the fly is fastened securely. This complicated maneuver takes just a fraction of a second, and is much too fast for the human eye to see.

BLOOD SUCKERS
The African tsetse fly feeds on the blood of mammals, including humans. Like many blood-sucking flies, it can spread diseases as it feeds.

LAYING EGGS
Within the space of a few seconds, a female blowfly leaves a batch of eggs on some rotting remains. Her eggs will produce blind, legless larvae called maggots.

AN AERIAL COURTSHIP
Hover flies can fly forwards, backwards and sideways, and are among the few insects that are able to hover for long periods. Here, a male courts a female by hovering above her.

UP, UP AND AWAY
Like their close relatives the mosquitoes, many midges spend the first part of life in pools and puddles. These newly emerged adult midges will soon take to the air.

STRANGE BUT TRUE
Before they mate, male dance flies present their partners with a tasty insect wrapped in silk. This gift keeps the female occupied during mating, and reduces the chance that she will attack the male. But some males cheat, and when their females unwrap the silk, they discover that there is nothing inside!

Discover more in A Closer View

True Bugs

People often use the word "bug" to mean any kind of insect, but true bugs are insects with mouthparts that pierce and suck. There are about 82,000 species of true bug, and while most live on land, some of the biggest and most ferocious live in lakes and ponds. Bugs use their piercing mouthparts to eat very different kinds of food. Some, including many water bugs, attack other animals. After stabbing them with their mouthparts, they suck out the nutritious fluids. Other bugs, including aphids, shield bugs and cicadas, live on plants and drink sugar-rich sap. Bugs hatch from eggs as nymphs, which are similar in shape to their parents. They molt up to six times before they become adults, and during this process, they often change color. Australian harlequin bugs (above) are bright orange when adult, but orange and steely blue as nymphs.

WALKING ON WATER
Pond-skaters are bugs with long legs that live on the water's surface. Here, several of them are feeding on a dead insect.

SMELLY PREY
When threatened, stink bugs produce pungent chemicals from glands near their back legs. Many, including this specimen from Borneo, are brightly colored to warn off birds.

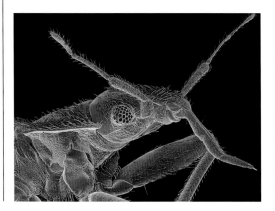

SLEEP WALKERS
Bedbugs use their piercing mouthparts to feed on human blood. They are active at night, but hide away in bedding and clothes during the day. Because of modern insecticides, they are becoming less common.

SNEAK ATTACK
The back swimmer swims upside down under the water, using its long back legs as oars. It pounces on insects that fall into the water and stabs them.

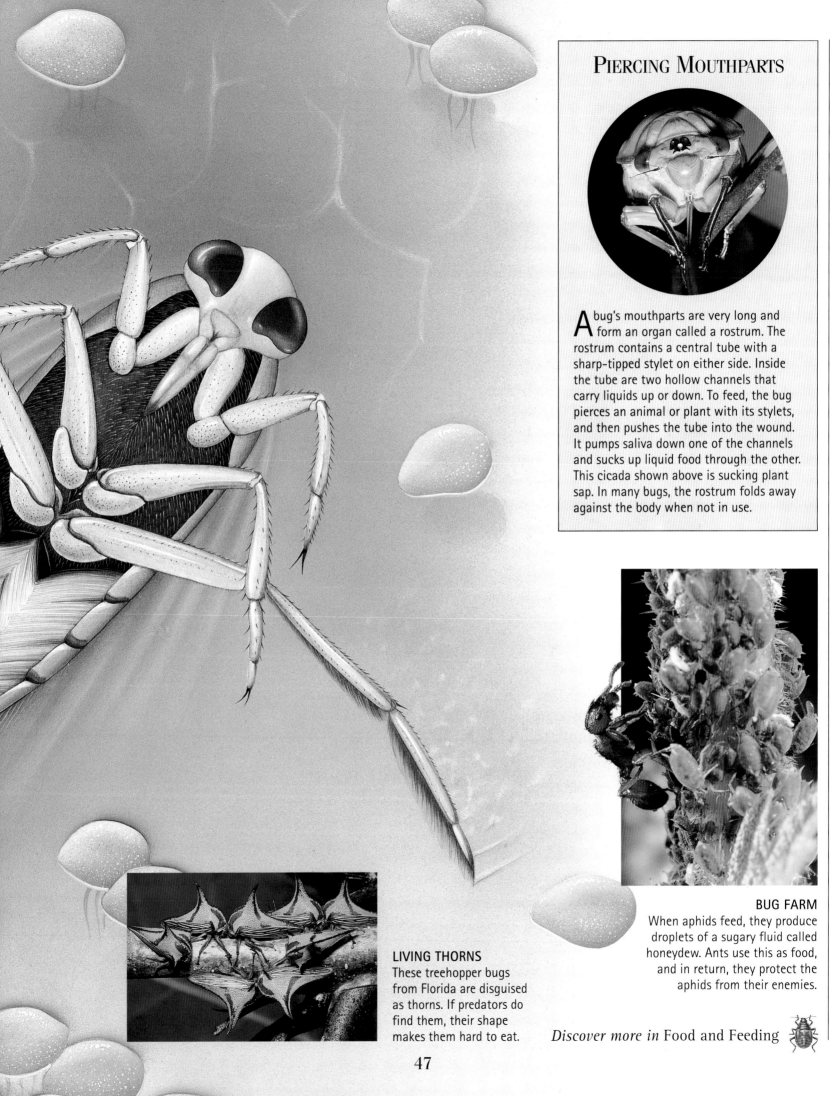

PIERCING MOUTHPARTS

A bug's mouthparts are very long and form an organ called a rostrum. The rostrum contains a central tube with a sharp-tipped stylet on either side. Inside the tube are two hollow channels that carry liquids up or down. To feed, the bug pierces an animal or plant with its stylets, and then pushes the tube into the wound. It pumps saliva down one of the channels and sucks up liquid food through the other. This cicada shown above is sucking plant sap. In many bugs, the rostrum folds away against the body when not in use.

BUG FARM
When aphids feed, they produce droplets of a sugary fluid called honeydew. Ants use this as food, and in return, they protect the aphids from their enemies.

LIVING THORNS
These treehopper bugs from Florida are disguised as thorns. If predators do find them, their shape makes them hard to eat.

Discover more in Food and Feeding

47

Insect Impact

Insects can both help and harm people. Without the ceaseless work of bees and other insects, many flowers would not be pollinated, and many of the plants we grow would not produce food. Without honeybees, there would be no honey, and without predatory insects, there would be many more pests. However, many of those pests are actually insects themselves. Caterpillars, bugs and beetles attack our crops, and in some parts of the world, swarms of locusts (a single locust is shown above) sometimes descend on fields, stripping them bare in less than an hour. Weevils bore their way through stored grain, beetles and termites tunnel through wood in houses and furniture, and some insects attack farm animals. Insects also harm us more directly. Some sting, but the most dangerous by far are those that carry diseases. Houseflies and cockroaches spread germs when they walk over our food, while mosquitoes, flies and fleas can infect us with germs when they feed on our blood.

NIGHT-TIME NUISANCE
Cockroaches feed at night, and eat anything from bread to shoe polish. They are very sensitive to vibrations, and scuttle away as soon as they sense danger.

WELCOME VISITORS
Many of the fruits and vegetables we eat have to be pollinated by insects before they will start to develop. Some fruit growers keep honeybees to pollinate their plants.

POTATO MENACE
The brightly colored Colorado beetle comes from North America. Originally, it fed on wild plants, but it now attacks potato plants in many parts of the world.

A DIET OF WOOL
The caterpillars of clothes moths often live in tiny silk bags, and feed on wool. They sometimes chew small holes in woolen clothes and blankets.

48

DEMOLITION SQUAD
Termites work in darkness, eating wood from the inside. The damage they cause is often hidden until the wood starts to collapse.

FATAL FLEAS
When fleas bite rats and then humans, they can pass on germs that cause the bubonic plague. In the 1300s, outbreaks of this disease killed millions of people.

THE DUNG-BEETLE STORY
Dung beetles are among our most unusual insect helpers. They dispose of animal manure (dung) by using it as food for their larvae. When early settlers imported cattle to Australia, the manure piled up, and the grass began to die. This was because Australian dung beetles were used to the droppings of native animals, but not to those of cattle. The solution to this problem was to bring in dung beetles from Africa, where wild cattle were common. Within a few years, they had cleared the manure away.

DID YOU KNOW?
The most serious disease spread by insects is malaria. It is carried by mosquitoes in their salivary glands. Since the Stone Age, malaria may have caused half of all human deaths. Today, it still kills between 2 and 4 million people every year.

MOUTHS ON THE MOVE
This swarm of hungry locusts in Africa spells disaster for farmers whose crops are in its path. Locusts normally live alone, but swarm when they are on the move.

Looking at Spiders

GIANT FANGS
These fangs stab downwards, pinning prey to the ground as the spider bites. Other spiders have fangs that come together when they bite.

With their hairy bodies and long legs, spiders provoke both fear and fascination. Like an insect, a spider has jointed legs and a hard body case, or carapace. But it differs from an insect in many other ways. Spiders belong to a group of animals called arachnids, which also includes scorpions, mites and ticks. Their bodies are divided into two parts separated by a slender waist, and they have eight legs rather than six. Spiders do not have antennae or wings, but they do have many eyes, and powerful jaws that can deliver a poisonous bite. All spiders are predators. Some eat frogs, lizards and even small birds, but most feed on insects. A spider uses its poisonous fluid, or venom, to paralyze its prey, and then injects it with digestive juices to dissolve the prey's tissue. The spider can then slowly suck it up. About 35,000 species of spider have been identified. They live in many different habitats, including forests, grasslands, caves, fresh water and our homes.

WATCHING FOR PREY
Most spiders have poor eyesight and sense the movement of prey through the hairs that cover their body and legs. This jumping spider however, has unusually good vision.

Leg
Each of a spider's eight legs is attached to the cephalothorax.

How Spiders Molt

In order to grow, spiders must periodically molt, or shed their hard outer skin. Just before it starts to molt, a spider hangs upside down and secures itself with a silk thread. Its skin splits around the sides of its cephalothorax and abdomen, and starts to fall away. Meanwhile, the spider pulls its legs out of the old skin, just like someone pulling their fingers out of a glove. When its body is free, it hangs from the thread, and expands to its new size.

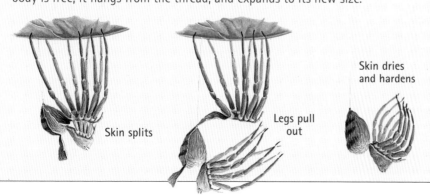

Skin splits

Legs pull out

Skin dries and hardens

BIRD KILLER
The largest spider in the world is the bird-eating spider, or tarantula, from South America. It can be as wide as 11 in (28 cm).

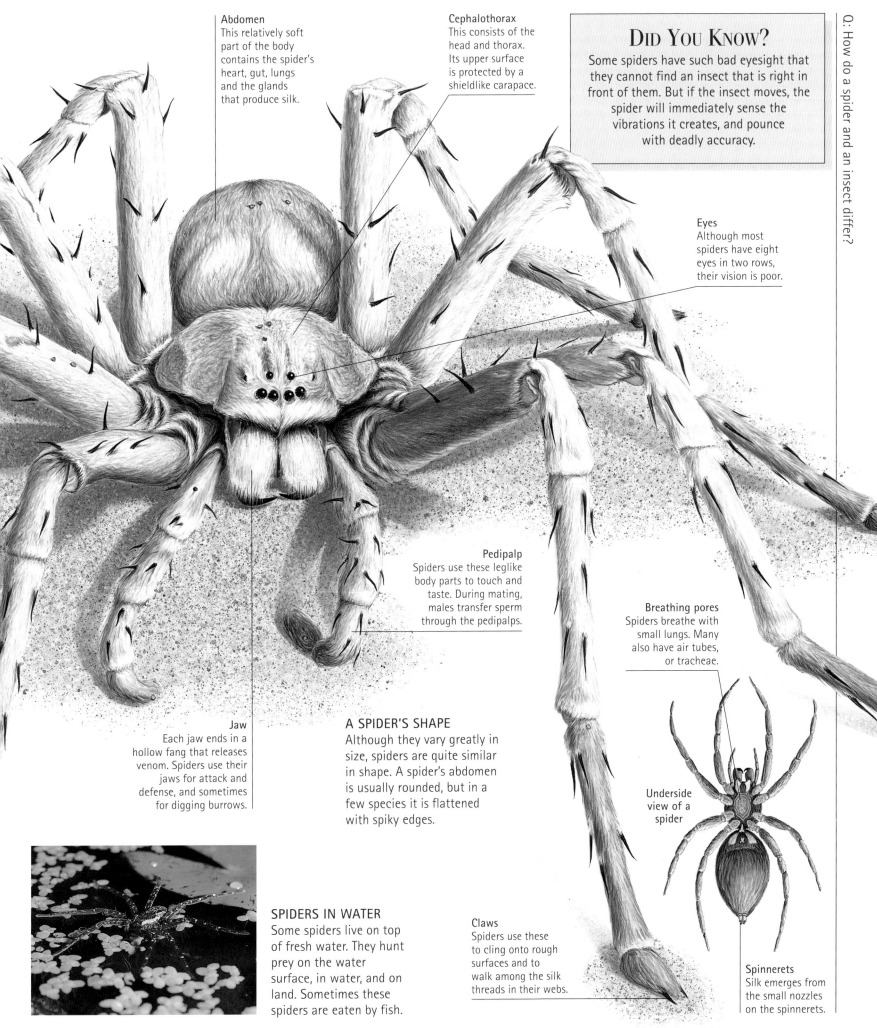

Abdomen
This relatively soft part of the body contains the spider's heart, gut, lungs and the glands that produce silk.

Cephalothorax
This consists of the head and thorax. Its upper surface is protected by a shieldlike carapace.

DID YOU KNOW?
Some spiders have such bad eyesight that they cannot find an insect that is right in front of them. But if the insect moves, the spider will immediately sense the vibrations it creates, and pounce with deadly accuracy.

Eyes
Although most spiders have eight eyes in two rows, their vision is poor.

Pedipalp
Spiders use these leglike body parts to touch and taste. During mating, males transfer sperm through the pedipalps.

Breathing pores
Spiders breathe with small lungs. Many also have air tubes, or tracheae.

Jaw
Each jaw ends in a hollow fang that releases venom. Spiders use their jaws for attack and defense, and sometimes for digging burrows.

A SPIDER'S SHAPE
Although they vary greatly in size, spiders are quite similar in shape. A spider's abdomen is usually rounded, but in a few species it is flattened with spiky edges.

Underside view of a spider

SPIDERS IN WATER
Some spiders live on top of fresh water. They hunt prey on the water surface, in water, and on land. Sometimes these spiders are eaten by fish.

Claws
Spiders use these to cling onto rough surfaces and to walk among the silk threads in their webs.

Spinnerets
Silk emerges from the small nozzles on the spinnerets.

51

Silk and Web Makers

Silk is a remarkable substance, made by all spiders and some insects. It starts out as a liquid, but can be turned into elastic strands that are sometimes stronger than steel. Spiders make different kinds of silk in special glands in their abdomens. The glands are connected to nozzles called spinnerets. As the liquid silk emerges from its spinnerets, a spider tugs it with its legs, which hardens the silk. For many spiders, the most important use of silk is in making webs. The shape of the web and the time spent building it depend on the species of spider. Once a web is complete, spiders usually lie in wait, either on the web itself or close enough to touch it with their legs. If anything makes the web vibrate, the spider instantly rushes out to investigate. If it discovers something edible, the spider often wraps up the victim with sticky threads before delivering a deadly bite.

FOOD PARCEL
This orb-web spider has caught a ladybug. To make sure victims cannot escape, they are wrapped in silk, which also prevents stinging insects from fighting back.

COMMUNAL WEBS
In warm parts of the world, some spiders cooperate to catch prey. This giant web in Papua New Guinea is several yards long. It was built by many spiders working together.

Hunting spider

DIFFERENT FEET
Spiders that hunt their prey usually have two claws on each foot, while spiders that trap their prey in webs have three. The central claw closes to grip the web.

Web-building spider

SPINNING SILK
Most spiders have three or four pairs of spinnerets. Here, several spinnerets work together as a spider builds its web.

OTHER USES OF SILK

Silk has many uses apart from making webs and wrapping up prey. Many spiderlings use silk to help them leave the nest and most spiders use it to produce a dragline, a thin silk thread that trails behind them as they move. With a dragline the spiders can lower themselves through the air, but winch themselves back up if they do not like what they find. Spiders also use silk for protecting their eggs and, as shown here, for making shelters. This jumping spider has used silk to fasten two leaves together as a temporary shelter.

PORTABLE TRAP
A net-throwing spider hangs upside down holding its web with its legs. If an insect walks beneath it, the spider stretches and lowers the web to scoop the prey up.

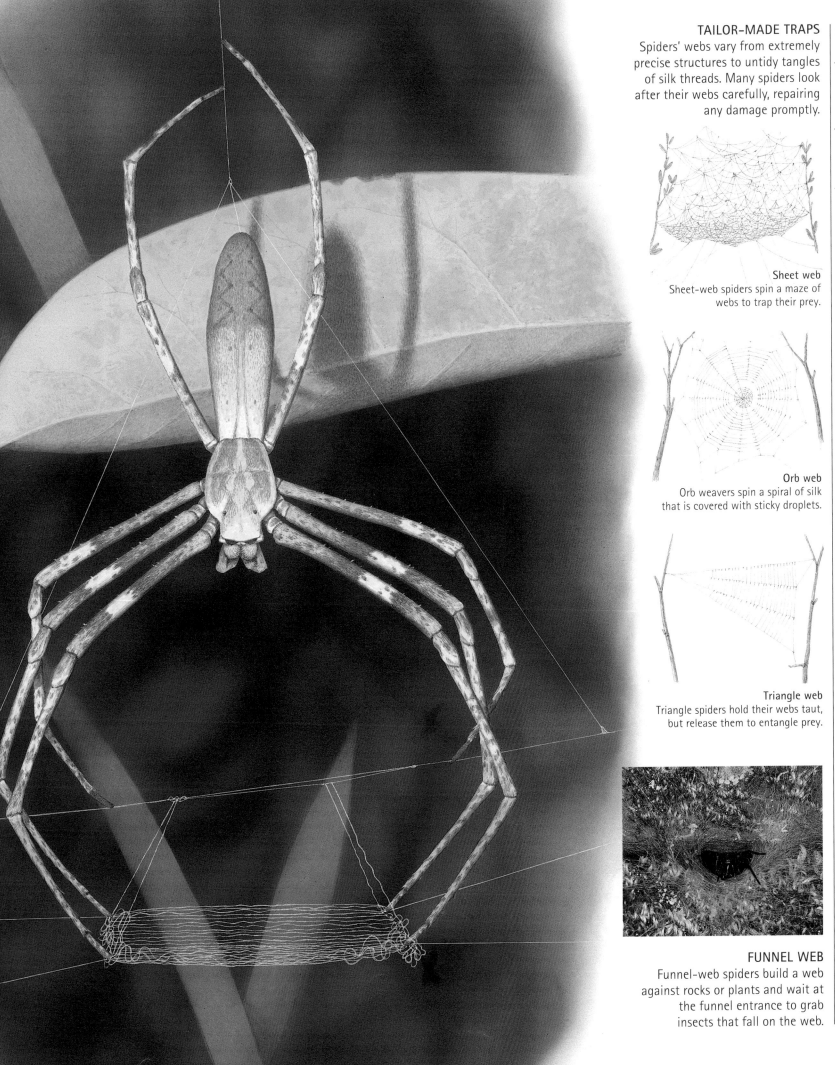

TAILOR-MADE TRAPS

Spiders' webs vary from extremely precise structures to untidy tangles of silk threads. Many spiders look after their webs carefully, repairing any damage promptly.

Sheet web

Sheet-web spiders spin a maze of webs to trap their prey.

Orb web

Orb weavers spin a spiral of silk that is covered with sticky droplets.

Triangle web

Triangle spiders hold their webs taut, but release them to entangle prey.

FUNNEL WEB

Funnel-web spiders build a web against rocks or plants and wait at the funnel entrance to grab insects that fall on the web.

HIDDEN HUNTERS

Camouflaged crab spiders keep quite still as they lurk among flowers with their front legs wide open. If a meal, such as a honeybee, lands within range, they strike instantly.

The Hunters

Not all spiders catch their prey with webs. Many use traps of a different kind, while others set off on patrol and pounce on anything that could make a meal. Spiders that trap their prey rely on disguise for a successful ambush. Crab spiders, for example, camouflage themselves and catch insects that land within reach. Trappers also include many species that build silk tubes, or tunnels with secret doors. If an unsuspecting insect wanders nearby, a trap-door spider flings open the door and lunges at its prey. Spiders that search for food operate either by day or by night. The busiest daytime hunters are the jumping spiders. They have extra-large eyes to help them find their prey. When the sun sets, the jumping spiders hide away, and much larger and more sinister-looking spiders, such as tarantulas, begin to emerge. Instead of hunting by sight, these spiders hunt by touch.

DEATH TRAP

This trap-door spider has opened its door wide, revealing the burrow beneath. Some trap doors are light and flimsy, but others contain earth as well as silk, and close under their own weight.

STRANGE BUT TRUE

At dusk, the bolas spider twirls a thread that ends in a drop of liquid silk. Male moths are attracted by a chemical in the silk, and become caught on the sticky blob. The spider then hauls in its prey.

SLIPPERY CATCH

Raft spiders hunt water animals by sensing the ripples the prey creates. After stabbing a fish with its fangs, this spider hauls its catch ashore.

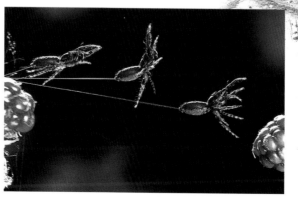

JUMPING ON PREY

Trailing its dragline, this sequence shows a jumping spider leaping through the air. This hunter can jump four times the length of its own body.

HUNTING UNDERWATER

The water spider survives in its unusual habitat by making a silk bubble, as shown below, to store air. It sits inside the air bubble and waits for prey to come along. If a small animal comes within range, the spider dashes out, attacks, and brings the victim back into the air bubble to be eaten. Water spiders also catch animals that have fallen onto the surface of the water, as well as search out prey on the muddy bottom of a pond. They find most of their food by detecting vibrations in the water.

NIGHT STALKERS
This rearing tarantula is more than a match for a mouse. Its diet can also include frogs, lizards, small birds and even young snakes.

Discover more in Predators and Parasites

INVISIBLE SPIDER
This Australian spider rests with its body sideways across a twig. Its dappled colors and knobbly abdomen make it look just like a ridge of bark.

ANT IMPOSTER
Many animals avoid ants because they can bite and sting. However, a close look shows that this tropical "ant" has eight legs. It is a spider in disguise.

PROTECTING EGGS
This spider (in the center) camouflages its egg sacs by disguising them as wrapped up prey. Other animals will be less interested in dead remains than in a spider's living eggs.

STRANGE BUT TRUE
Predatory animals are not interested in bird droppings, so looking like a bird dropping is a very effective disguise. Spiders that imitate droppings usually rest on leaves, and their bodies are often shiny, which makes them look wet.

• SPOTLIGHT ON SPIDERS •

Spider Defense

Spiders are very effective hunters, but sometimes they can become the hunted. Their enemies are numerous, and include birds, lizards, frogs, toads, centipedes and deadly hunting wasps. These wasps paralyze spiders by stinging them, and use the still-living spider as food for their young. To outwit their enemies, spiders use a range of defenses. Many are camouflaged to blend in with their backgrounds, while some imitate things that are not normally eaten. Others hide away in burrows topped with trap doors, and hold their doors firmly shut if an enemy tries to break in. If this tactic fails and the door is forced open, the owner often retreats into a hidden chamber behind a further door. It remains here until the danger has passed. Despite these defenses, many spiders are killed. Their best resource in the struggle for survival, however, is that most species lay a large number of eggs, so although many die, some always manage to survive.

NASTY SHOWER
A tarantula's hairs have microscopic barbed spines that can make skin itch and burn. When threatened, a tarantula scrapes hairs off its abdomen and showers them on its enemy.

EGG FACTORY
A single garden spider can produce more than 500 eggs. Garden spiders live in the open and are easy prey, so only a few of the spiderlings survive to become adults.

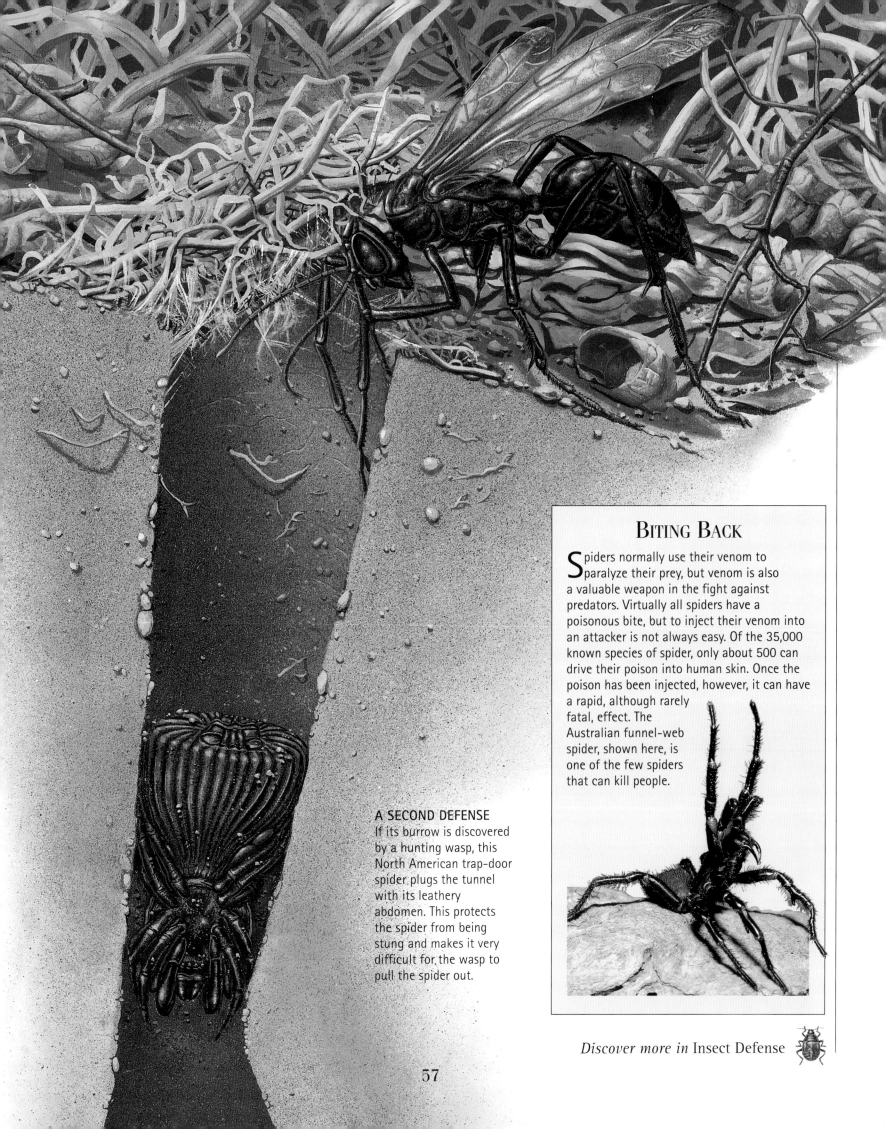

BITING BACK

Spiders normally use their venom to paralyze their prey, but venom is also a valuable weapon in the fight against predators. Virtually all spiders have a poisonous bite, but to inject their venom into an attacker is not always easy. Of the 35,000 known species of spider, only about 500 can drive their poison into human skin. Once the poison has been injected, however, it can have a rapid, although rarely fatal, effect. The Australian funnel-web spider, shown here, is one of the few spiders that can kill people.

A SECOND DEFENSE

If its burrow is discovered by a hunting wasp, this North American trap-door spider plugs the tunnel with its leathery abdomen. This protects the spider from being stung and makes it very difficult for the wasp to pull the spider out.

Discover more in Insect Defense

New Life

BREAKING OUT
Most spiderlings molt for the first time while still safe inside the egg sac. After molting, they break through the silk into the world outside.

Before spiders can reproduce, males and females have to come together to mate. For a male, mating can be a dangerous activity, because he needs to be cautious to avoid being attacked by the female. Once mating has taken place, the male's work is done. Maternal care varies among different species of female spider. However, they all wrap their eggs in a silk bundle called an egg sac, and either hide the sac somewhere safe, or carry it with them as they hunt. Young spiders, or spiderlings, look like miniature versions of their parents. They break out of the egg sac soon after they hatch, and at first cling either to each other, or to their mother's body. A few female spiders find food for their young, but eventually they have to catch food for themselves. From then on each spiderling is on its own.

HITCHING A RIDE
A female wolf spider's egg sac is attached to her spinnerets, and she often warms it in the sunshine (above left). When her spiderlings hatch, they climb onto the top of her abdomen.

LONG LIFE
Guarded by their mother, young tarantulas explore the outside world. Tropical tarantulas are the longest living of all spiders.

TREADING LIGHTLY

Most spiders live alone and do not like to be approached. This creates problems for male spiders, because they could be attacked when they try to court females. The males avoid this fate by using signals. In species that have good eyesight, the male waves its legs or its pedipalps in a special sequence. Web-building spiders often have poor eyesight, so the male (far left) has to use another signaling technique. This spider tugs on the female's web as it carefully makes its approach.

UNEQUAL PARTNERS
Many male spiders are much smaller than the female. Here a male spider hesitantly advances towards his gigantic, and perhaps hungry, mate.

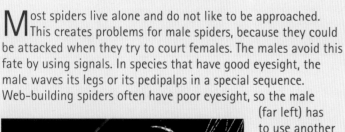

SECURITY BLANKET
Orb-weaving spiders often cover their egg sac with a blanket of tough silk. This makes it more difficult for predators and parasites to reach the eggs.

FLYING AWAY
To leave the nest, many species of spider use threads of silk as sails to launch themselves into the wind from the tops of plants (far left). When moving around the plants, the spiderlings use draglines as shown below.

STRANGE BUT TRUE
Many female spiders die after they have laid their eggs. For some spiderlings, the mother's body is their first meal. They feed on her remains before setting off to catch food for themselves.

Orders of Insects & Spiders

Scientists arrange living things in groups to show how they are related through evolution. The largest groups are called kingdoms, and the smallest are called species. In between, there are classes, orders, suborders, families and genera. Each species consists of living things that breed together, and each one has its own two-part scientific name. So far, scientists have identified and named more than 2 million species of living things. Of these, only about 45,000 are vertebrates (animals with backbones) while more than 1 million are arthropods, which include insects and spiders. The species totals shown on these two pages are recent estimates, but it is certain that many more insects and spiders await discovery.

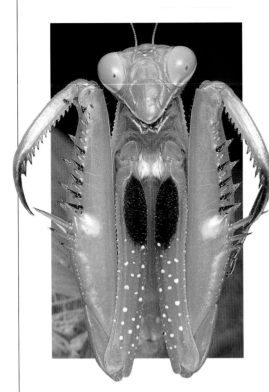

READY TO STRIKE
With its stabbing forelegs raised and ready to strike, this mantis looks like someone at prayer. It belongs to the order Mantodea.

TWO WINGS
Like all other species in the order Diptera, this greenbottle fly has just a single pair of wings. It is a fast and noisy flier.

INSECTS
Class: Insecta

Main insect orders	Meaning of order name	Estimated no. of species	Examples
Coleoptera	hard wings	400,000	beetles, cockchafers, fireflies, ladybugs, weevils
Lepidoptera	scaly wings	150,000	butterflies, moths
Hymenoptera	membrane wings	130,000	ants, bees, wasps
Diptera	two wings	120,000	true flies, hover flies, midges, mosquitoes
Hemiptera	half wings	82,000	aphids, bugs, cicadas, pond-skaters, water boatmen, back swimmers, water scorpions
Orthoptera	straight wings	20,500	crickets, grasshoppers, locusts
Trichoptera	hairy wings	10,000	caddis flies
Collembola	sticky peg	6,000	springtails
Odonata	toothed flies	5,500	damselflies, dragonflies
Neuroptera	net-veined wings	5,000	lacewings
Thysanoptera	fringed wings	5,000	thrips
Blattodea	insect avoiding light	3,700	cockroaches
Pscoptera	milled wings	3,200	booklice, woodlice
Phthiraptera	louse wings	3,000	biting and sucking lice
Phasmatodea	like a ghost	2,500	leaf insects, stick insects
Siphonaptera	tube without wings	2,400	fleas
Isoptera	equal wings	2,300	termites
Ephemeroptera	living for a day	2,100	mayflies
Plecoptera	wickerwork wings	2,000	stoneflies
Dermaptera	leathery wings	1,800	earwigs
Mantodea	like a prophet	1,800	praying mantises
Mecoptera	long wings	400	scorpion flies
Thysanura	bristle tails	370	silverfish

BITING JAWS
These formidable jaws that bite downwards belong to a mygalomorph spider, which is a member of the suborder Orthognatha.

TRUE SPIDERS
These sideways-biting jaws belong to a true spider, from the suborder Labidognatha. This large group includes the vast majority of the world's spiders.

SPIDERS
Class: Arachnida

Spider order
Araneae

Suborder	Distinctive features	No. of families	Estimated no. of species	Examples and family name
Labidognatha (true spiders)	Their jaws are attached below the head and bite from side to side.	90	32,000	jumping spiders (Salticidae) sheet-web weavers (Linyphiidae) orb weavers (Argiopidae) wolf spiders (Lycosidae) crab spiders (Thomisidae) funnel-web spiders (Agelenidae)
Orthognatha (mygalomorph spiders)	Their jaws bite forwards and down.	15	3,000	tarantulas (Theraphosidae)
Mesothelae (primitive, segmented spiders)	Their abdomens have several segments, like those of insects.	1	24	segmented spiders (Liphistiidae)

HARD WINGS
This scarab beetle belongs to the biggest order, Coleoptera. Its back wings are protected by hard front wings when it clambers across the ground.

STRAIGHT WINGS
Bush crickets belong to the order Orthoptera. Like grasshoppers, they have straight wings, and the front pair is often hard and leathery.

SCALY WINGS
This birdwing butterfly belongs to the order Lepidoptera. Its wings and body are covered with a huge number of tiny, but brightly colored scales.

61

Glossary

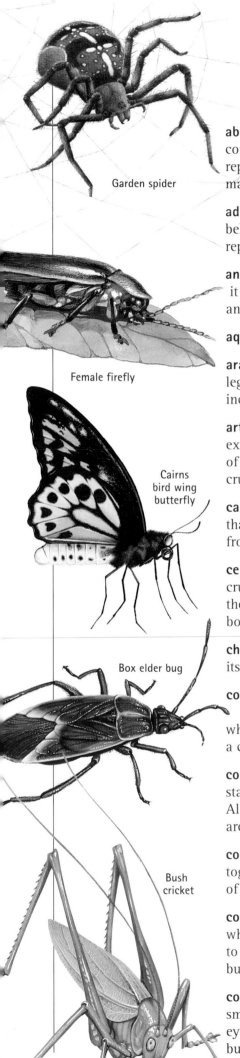

Garden spider

Female firefly

Cairns bird wing butterfly

Box elder bug

Bush cricket

abdomen The part of an animal's body that contains the digestive system and the organs of reproduction. In insects and spiders, the abdomen makes up the rear of the body.

adaptation A change that occurs in an animal's behavior or body to allow it to survive and reproduce in new conditions.

antenna A slender organ on an animal's head that it uses to sense its surroundings. Insects have two antennae, which are often known as "feelers."

aquatic Living all or most of the time in water.

arachnid An arthropod with four pairs of walking legs. Arachnids make up the class Arachnida, and include spiders, scorpions, mites and ticks.

arthropod An animal with jointed legs and a hard exoskeleton. Arthropods make up the largest group of animals on Earth and include insects, spiders, crustaceans, centipedes and millipedes.

camouflage The colors and patterns of an animal that blend in with the background and conceal it from predators and help it to ambush prey.

cephalothorax In spiders, other arachnids and crustaceans, a region of the body that combines the head and thorax. It is covered by a hard body case.

chitin A hard substance that gives an exoskeleton its strength.

cocoon A protective case made of silk. Many insects use cocoons to protect themselves while they are pupae. Female spiders often spin a cocoon to protect their eggs.

cold-blooded Not able to keep the body at a stable, warm temperature by internal means. All arthropods, including insects and spiders, are cold-blooded.

colony A group of closely related animals that live together. Many insect colonies consist of a family of animals produced by a single queen.

complete metamorphosis A way of developing in which a young insect changes shape from an egg to a larva, to a pupa, to an adult. Beetles and butterflies develop by complete metamorphosis.

compound eye An eye that is divided into many smaller eyes, each with its own lens. Compound eyes are found in most insects and crustaceans, but not in spiders.

display A series of movements that animals use to communicate with their own kind, or with other animals. Displays often signal that an animal is ready to attack, or to mate.

dragline A slender strand of silk that spiders leave behind them when they move about.

drone A male honeybee. Drones mate with young queens, but unlike worker bees, they do not help in collecting food or maintaining a hive.

egg sac A silk bag that some spiders spin around their eggs. Some egg sacs are portable, so the eggs can be carried from place to place. Others are more like a blanket.

evolution The gradual change, over many generations, in plant or animal species as they adapt to new conditions or new environments.

exoskeleton A hard external skeleton, or body case, that protects an animal's body. All arthropods are protected in this way.

eyelet One of the small eyes that form part of a larger compound eye. An eyelet senses light from the animal's surroundings.

ganglion A cluster of nerve cells that does not form part of the brain. In many invertebrates, ganglia control different parts of the body.

gills Organs that collect oxygen from water. Gills are found in many aquatic animals, including fish and some insects.

grub An insect larva.

habitat The home of an animal or plant. Many different kinds of insects live in the same environment, but each kind lives in a different habitat within that environment.

haltere One of a pair of the modified back wings of a fly. They help the fly to balance during flight.

hibernate To remain completely inactive during the cold winter months. Insects hibernate as either eggs, larvae, pupae or adults.

incomplete metamorphosis A way of developing in which a young insect gradually changes shape from an egg to a nymph, to an adult.

invertebrate An animal that does not have a backbone. Some invertebrates are soft-bodied, but others, including insects, are protected by hard body cases.

larva A young animal that looks completely different from its parents. Insect larvae change into adults by complete metamorphosis. A larva is sometimes called a grub.

lift The upward force that helps flying animals to stay in the air. Lift is produced when air flows over the wings.

metamorphosis A way of developing in which an animal's body changes shape. Many invertebrates, including insects, undergo metamorphosis as they mature.

migration A seasonal journey to a place with a more suitable climate. Some flying insects migrate hundreds of miles to a warmer climate to mate and lay eggs. They may die there, but sometimes their offspring return to the place of origin.

molt To shed an outer layer of the body. Insects molt by shedding their outer skins, while birds molt by shedding their feathers.

nerve cord The part of an insect's nervous system that carries signals between its body and brain.

nymph The young stage of an insect that develops by incomplete metamorphosis. Nymphs are often similar to adults, but do not have fully developed wings.

ocellus A simple kind of eye with a single lens. Insects have three ocelli on the top of their head.

order A major group that biologists use when classifying living things. An order is divided into smaller groups from suborders to families, to genera and finally to species.

ovipositor A tubelike organ through which female insects lay their eggs. The stings of bees and wasps are modified ovipositors.

palp or pedipalp One of a pair of small, leglike organs on the head of insects, spiders and other arthropods, used for feeling or handling food. In spiders, the pedipalps are also used for mating.

pheromone A chemical released by one animal that affects the behavior of others. Many insects use pheromones to attract mates, or to signal danger.

pollen A dustlike substance produced by male flowers or the male organs in a flower, and used in reproduction.

predator An animal that lives mainly by killing and eating other animals.

proboscis In insects, a long mouthpart or tongue used for feeding.

proleg A sucker-like leg in caterpillars. Prolegs disappear when a caterpillar turns into an adult butterfly or moth.

queen A female insect that begins a social insect colony. The queen is normally the only member of the colony that lays eggs.

silk A strong but elastic substance produced by many insects and spiders. Silk is liquid until it leaves the animal's body.

social insect An insect that lives in large family groups.

spinneret An organ that spiders use to produce their silk. The spinnerets are near the tip of a spider's abdomen.

spiracle A round opening that leads into an insect's trachea, or breathing tube.

stridulate To make a sound by scraping things together. Many insects communicate in this way by scraping their legs against their body.

stylet A sharp mouthpart used for piercing plants or animals.

thorax The middle part of an animal's body. In insects, the thorax is divided from the head by a narrow "neck." In spiders, the thorax and head make up a single unit.

tissue A part of an organism made up of a large number of cells that have a similar structure and function.

trachea A breathing tube in an animal's body. In vertebrates, there is one trachea and it leads to the lungs. Insects have many small tracheae that spread throughout their body.

venomous Describes a creature that is poisonous and that can attack other animals. Venomous animals usually attack by biting or stinging.

vertebrate An animal with a backbone. Vertebrates include fish, amphibians, reptiles, birds and mammals.

warm-blooded Able to keep the internal body temperature more or less stable by internal means.

worker A social insect that collects food and tends a colony's young, but which usually cannot reproduce.

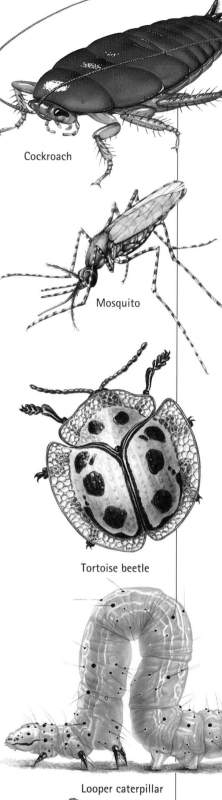

Cockroach

Mosquito

Tortoise beetle

Looper caterpillar

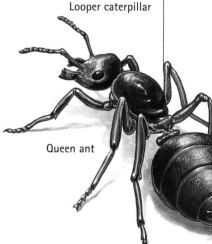

Queen ant

63

Index

Picture Credits

(t=top, b=bottom, l=left, r=right, c=center, F=front, C=cover, B=back, Bg=background)
Ardea, 48c (I.R. Beames), 30bl (J. Daniels), 40br (A. Warren). Kathie Atkinson, 26bl, 51bl, 56tl. Auscape, 9tl (K. Atkinson), 42c, (J. Cancalosi), 46tl, 52cr, 61bc (J.P. Ferrero), 14tl, 31br, 58cr, 61cl, 61tl (P. Goetgheluck P.H.O.N.E.), 48/49c (Helio/Van Ingen), 23tcr, (C.A. Henley), 23bcr, 28bl (R. Morrison), 27bl (A. & J. Six), 60bl (J. Six), 61cr (G. Threlfo). Austral International, 42tl (R. Amann/Sygma), 50br (D. Heuclin/SIPA Press), 16bc, 31bl (H. Pfletschinger/Camera Press). Australian Picture Library, 52br (M. Moffett/Minden Pictures). Dr Hans Bänziger, 41br. Bruce Coleman Limited, 29tr (J. Brackenbury), 16tl, 18bl, 53br, 58bl (J. Burton), 47bl (J. Cancalosi), 56br (R.P. Carr), 25tl (G. Dore), 36tl (M.P.L. Fogden), 50cl (F. Labhardt), 39t (G. McCarthy), 28br, 38br (Dr E. Pott), 57br (F. Prenzel), 27c (Dr S. Prato), 32c, 52bl, 60tl (Dr F. Sauer), 50tr, 58tr (A. Stillwell), 19bl, 20cl, 23tr, 23br, 47br, 54bc (K. Taylor), 34cl (P. Ward). CSIRO Division of Entomology, 48r (J. Green), 13b (Melbourne University Press). Ellis Nature Photography, 46cl. Pavel German, 56tc. Mantis Wildlife, 11cr, 24l, 26cl, 39br, 43tr, 47tr (D. Clyne), 58br (J. Frazier). Mary

Evans Picture Library, 49tc. NHM Picture Library, 6tr, 6bl, 11tc (The Natural History Museum, London). NHPA, 14c, 22tl (A. Bannister), 44cl, 56bl (G.I. Bernard), 32br (S. Dalton). Oxford Scientific Films, 9br, 22cl, 55r (G.I. Bernard), 17tl (S. Camazine), 43tl, 49tl, 56bc, 59tl (J.A.L. Cooke), 21cr, 54cl (D. Fox). 15tr, 31tl (London Scientific Films), 54bl (A. Ramage), 37br (K.B. Sandved), 6br (D. Shale), 34bl (H. Taylor Abipp). Nature Focus, 10br, 11tr (Australian Museum). Charles Palek, 6tl. The Photo Library, Sydney, 14bcr, 30tr, 45tr (Dr J. Burgess/SPL), 24tr (C. Cooper), 44bc (M. Dohrn/SPL), 38t (M. Kage/SPL), 10bl, 14br, 14bl, 20tl (Nuridsany & Perennou/SPL), 40tr, (A. Pasieka/SPL), 21tl (J.H. Robinson), 8br, 13tr, 14bcl, 46bl D. Scharf/SPL), 18c (SPL), 11tl (A. Syred/SPL). Planet Earth Pictures, 48bc (J. Downer), 41bl, 46c (G. du Feu), 11bl, 42bl, 52tr, (S. Hopkin), 16br, 21tr (B. Kenney), 23tl (K. Lucas), 12bc, 12br (J. Lythgoe), 48tr (J. & G. Lythgoe), 18cl (D. Maitland). Premaphotos Wildlife, 17tr, 20bl, 22bl, 40c, 44c, 56cl (K.G. Preston-Mafham). Terra Australis Photo Agency, 31tr, 45br (E. Beaton).

Illustration Credits

Susanna Addario, 3, 30tl, 30cr, 42/43b, 42tr, 63bcr. Martin Camm, 18tl, 18br, 19t. Simone End, 1, 7br, 7bc, 29br, 29bc, 29bl, 35l, 37bl, 38bc, 38bl, 63cr, icons. Christer Eriksson, 5br, 6/7c, 15br, 16bl, 28/29c, 30/31c, 35/38c, 54/55c, 61tr, 62tl. Giuliano Fornari, 52cl, 53c, 53cr, 53tr, 53tcr. Jon Gittoes, 46/47c. Ray Grinaway, 4tl, 5tl, 5cr, 7c, 14tc, 14cl, 15tl, 28/29t, 28cl, 28c (J. Brackenbury/Cassell), 40bl, 40tcl, 40bcl, 40tl, 44bl, 54tl, 54c, 62cl. Tim Hayward/Bernard Thornton Artists, UK, 22/23c, 22c, 58/59c, 58cl, 63br. Robert Hynes, 20/21c, 21br, 34/39c, 34tl, 39tr, 39cr. David Kirshner, 8/9c, 8bl, 9tr, 10/11c. Frank Knight, 26/27t, 27br. James McKinnon, 56/57c. John Richards, 32/33c, 32bc, 32cl, 32tl, 33b, 62tcl. Trevor Ruth, 2, 40/41c, 41tr, 41cr, 44tl, 44/45c. Claudia Saraceni, 4/5bc, 16/17c, 17r, 48tl, 48bl, 49bl, 63tcr. Kevin Stead, 4bl, 5tr, 12/13c, 12l, 13r, 19br, 24/25c, 24b, 25tcl, 25tcl, 25tr, 32bl, 62bcl, 62bl, 63tr. Thomas Trojer, 50/51c, 50bl, 51br. Rod Westblade, endpapers.

Cover Credits

Susanna Addario, BCbr. Martin Camm, FCtl. Richard Davies, Bg. Christer Eriksson, FCtr, FCbc. David Kirshner, BCtl.